When Your Child Asks

Books by Simon Glustrom

When Your Child Asks

Living with Your Teenager

The Language of Judaism

The Myth and Reality of Judaism

When Your Child Asks

by *Simon Glustrom*

A HANDBOOK FOR JEWISH PARENTS

NEW YORK

Bloch Publishing Company

Manufactured in the United States of America

Library of Congress Cataloging-in-Publication Data

Glustrom, Simon
    When your child asks : a handbook for Jewish parents / by Simon
Glustrom
        p. cm.
    Includes index.
    ISBN 0-8197-0571-3 (pbk.) : $10.95
    1. Judaism—Study and teaching. I. Title.   91-14423
    296.7'8—dc20   CIP

To

HELEN

JAN SHIRA

BETH ORA

ALIZA JO

Acknowlegements

To the many members of the Fair Lawn Jewish Center who have consistently asked probing questions about Judaism and encouraged their children to bring their questions to me, I owe the concept of and inspiration for this volume. I continue to remember with much fondness Dr. Solomon Grayzel and Dr. Abraham Millgram for their encouragement and keen insights which they contributed so freely when I was preparing this book for its original publication. Rabbis Max Arzt and Theodore Friedman also offered many helpful and stimulating suggestions at that time. I was also fortunate to have worked with Lily Edelman, who provided invaluable editorial help.

I am deeply indebted to Ilene McGrath, who edited this revised edition with care and skill. I wish to express my gratitude to my long-time friend, Charles Bloch, who enthusiastically agreed to republish this volume for a new generation of parents and children.

Preface

A parent would have to be extremely keen to detect the daily physical growth of his or her child. But the same parent can notice, without too much difficulty, the child's daily intellectual and emotional development, detecting in the child's questions a deepening curiosity as to the meaning of life and his relationship to the world. Every time the child asks a question he or she is trying to match another piece of the cosmic jig-saw puzzle.

Almost all parents are anxious to provide their children with the physical necessities of life—shelter, food, and clothing. And most of us know that love is indispensable to the child's security and happiness.

But many of us stop there. We are often content to shift responsibility for the education and religious training of our children to the professionals in school or synagogue who, we feel, are specially trained to teach the young. Many fathers and mothers develop a sense of inferiority to their child's teachers, in the belief that the teachers are better qualified than they to give counsel.

Even before the child reaches school age, during the third or fourth year, when he reaches the "why" stage of development, parents often begin to feel inadequate. They realize that they have given little or no thought to many of the questions the child asks. It would be much simpler if the youngster postponed such questions at least until entering school, when more qualified teachers could take over. But children are seldom that obliging. They inquire because of an urgent need to satisfy their curiosity.

In the light of studies in psychology, it is almost needless to emphasize that the attitudes which the young child formulates will have a significant effect upon later development. To withhold vital answers is to deny spiritual and intellectual nourishment when it is most needed.

We cannot be expected to know all the answers, nor to be equipped with all the insights of child psychology. Just as we need not feel guilty because of our inability to answer intricate questions about astronomy or biology, so is there no reason to feel pangs of conscience for not being experts in the field of Jewish learning. We should, however, be in a position to introduce to our children at least some of the basic Jewish ideas and values that impact upon our lives. To fulfill that task, we too must possess the curiosity of our children. The principle of learning in order to teach, expressed by an ancient sage, is as relevant today as when it was first pronounced.

Jewish parents' explanations should also include Jewish rituals and holidays, and how to deal with anti-Semitism. Children become aware of differences at a very early age, sometimes even before they start school. Learning that they are unlike their friends in certain ways can bring a great deal of unhappiness, especially if being a Jew is merely a label rather than a meaningful way of living. That is why it is of prime importance that the parent teach the child, first by example and later by precept, a sense of self-esteem and personal worth in belonging to the Jewish group.

This book addresses itself to the many parents whose children seek answers about Judaism. It is not intended to cover the field of Jewish theology. Rather, it is an attempt to discuss some of the basic Jewish concepts and problems that are of concern to children from age five into the teens.

A word on the format of the book. Each chapter is divided into two sections: the first provides background material for the parent; the second contains relevant questions, many of which were actually asked by children in the Religious School of the Fair Lawn Jewish Center over a period of years. The purpose of this division is twofold: to inform those who are not necessarily prompted by special questions but are interested in the general subject, and to assist the parent who is seeking answers to specific types of questions on Judaism that children ask. The question and answer method is intended merely to suggest to the parent possible ways of replying. It is understood, of course, that the child's questions may be phrased in different ways and that the answers will vary according to the child's mental capacity, Jewish background, and extent of interest in the subject. Little will be gained if the child is asked merely to read the answer himself, for it is only the live, human element injected by the parent that can, in the final analysis, encourage the child to inquire further about the meaning of the Jewish heritage. Much of the child's attitude toward Judaism will inevitably be shaped by that of the parents.

I shall be grateful to readers for their suggestions, criticisms, and experiences with this handbook so that in the future I may continue to serve the needs of Jewish parents and their children.

Fair Lawn, New Jersey

Simon Glustrom

Contents

Facts Are Not Enough:

Helpful Suggestions to Parents

Before considering some of the basic problems that confront our children, we must realize that our approach is very important. *How* we answer can be as vital as *what* we answer.

By observing the following "do's", parents may make their responses more effective and thus help to encourage further inquiry.

Do show interest. The extent of interest that you show in your child's question is of utmost significance. The parent who is intent only upon quieting the child for the moment may be giving the message that the subject is not worthy of further discussion.

It is understandable that parents are not necessarily prepared or able to sit down and discuss religious and social questions whenever their children happen to ask them. A parent who has just returned from a busy day at the office, for example, is entitled to relax for a while. However, a reply such as "Let's talk about it before bedtime" will go a long way in showing the child that you are pleased with the question and regard it as important enough for discussion at a more

1

suitable time.

Do encourage questions. There are many ways in which parents may arouse curiosity in children. Stimulating conversation at the dinner table and inviting the child's participation will further the desire to learn. You can also encourage inquiry by bringing interesting books and articles to your child's attention and by discussing and analyzing good movies and television programs. In short, interested parents develop curious children.

Do show consistency. Children cannot expect parents to know all the answers about Judaism, but they should be able to look to them for consistency in the knowledge that they do possess. This does not mean that you cannot change your opinion or correct an erroneous impression that you may have given. However, if you are to make your answers convincing, they should follow a logical pattern.

Consistency between parents is also important. Husband and wife may come from different religious backgrounds and their opinions about Judaism may differ considerably. They should not be expected to submerge their individualities for the sake of unity, yet it is not difficult to imagine how confused the child can become if each parent attempts to win the child over to a different and conflicting point of view. Parents rather should stress those points of agreement between them, and their differences of opinion should be presented in such a way that the child can eventually choose between two relative goods.

Now let us consider what the parent should avoid:

Don't argue with your child. You are not engaging in a debate with him, nor should you display your superior mentality by "forcing the child into a corner." Authority may win an argument, but you may lose the child's confidence and interest. In the future he or she may keep silent in order to avoid being overwhelmed.

Don't give pat answers. When children ask about Judaism, parents can be most effective by helping them arrive at their own conclusions. The old Socratic method of helping the child formulate the answer will ensure greater interest and retention. An answer in the form of a catechism may simplify the task, but something important is lost–the opportunity to develop the child's mind and have the child associate Judaism with the spirit of inquiry and reason.

Don't give the child more than he or she can digest at one time. If a young child asks why the postman brings the mail, you would hardly try to impress him with your knowledge of the Civil Service. You might say, "It is his job to deliver letters that people write us. That is his way of making a living and he is doing a very important job for us." We likewise answer the questions about God or death concisely and simply, paving the way for further questions at other times.

Don't teach the child false ideas that will later have to be unlearned. You should be helping the child to build upon a simple foundation of truth as he or she matures. That is why God should never be represented as a man, even to four-year-olds. Birth should not be identified with storks, nor death with a trip to Hawaii. When the child becomes aware of these untruthful explanations he may lose faith in the idea that was taught to him, and in his teacher as well.

GOD: THE JEWISH VIEW
"TELL ME ABOUT GOD"

GOD: THE JEWISH VIEW

Ever since people first conceived of God's existence, they have attempted to understand His true essence. We have come a long way from the time when God was thought of as a power that merely served our personal needs or those of a particular group of people. As humans' minds have developed, so has their concept of God.

However, our knowledge of God will never be complete, since it is impossible for a finite mind to comprehend the Infinite. We can only attempt to understand what He is like by observing how He has made Himself manifest in the world about us and in the days before us.

God's presence is manifest in the world of nature. Not only did He create the world but He continues to renew the work of creation. The changing of seasons, the rebirth of plant life, the creation of animal and human life are the result of God's will. Unlike the deist, who claims that God created the world and left it unattended, Judaism claims that without His constant attention the world could not endure. The design and purpose in the movements of even the least developed animals, and the economy in the world of nature, seem to indicate a guiding force and purposive mind behind it all.

Judaism believes that God also operated through history. Events did not just happen; there is a pattern and purpose to the course of events. Even the Egyptian bondage and the Jewish exile into Babylonia were intended to serve a divine purpose. That weaker nations often prevailed over stronger ones because the former were more ethical was attributed to God's influence in the shaping of history. Because of His role in history, He is frequently referred to as God of the Patriarchs, of the Exodus, and of Sinai.

Judaism has time and again emphasized that fulfillment of God's law is preferred to a mere statement of faith. To contend merely that we have faith in God signifies little, especially since there is not necessarily a correlation between what a person claims to believe and what that person does. Jewish scholars have indicated that the ancient Jews did not even discuss the existence of God—they took it for granted. In the Bible one finds no speculation concerning the reality of God. The prophets may have questioned His justice from time to time but they did not speculate on God's existence. The Jew was primarily interested in doing God's will. Deed took precedence over creed.

Concepts of the God Idea in Judaism

God Is One. The unity of God is one of the most significant contributions that Judaism has made to the world. Today some of the major religions believe in monotheism, but for centuries the Jews stood alone against the whole world in their insistence upon one God.

To contend that God is One is not the simple statement that it appears to be on the surface. It does more than simply deny belief in many gods. God, who is One, is the source of goodness in the world. He is the Supreme God of morality and to Him alone is to be directed the unconditional loyalty of humans. In pagan and other religions, people worshipped many gods, each representing specific attributes. For example, the Greeks had gods of war, love; wisdom, and many others. In monotheism one God represents all of the ideals combined. People are expected to pursue not one narrow ideal as a goal in life but all the ideals that the *one* God represents.

Belief in monotheism also demands that people regard the human race as one. If one God is the Father of us all, then it follows that all humans are members of one family. To injure another human being is to harm one's own flesh and blood. It is this belief in the Fatherhood of God and brotherhood of humanity that inspired the prophet to ask:

> Have we not all one Father? Has not one God created us?
> Why do we deal treacherously, a man against his brother?

Belief in monotheism further means that all social classes within a society are subject to His moral law. It serves to reject any twofold moral code—one for the ruler and another for the ruled, one for the strong and another for the weak. It is the belief in ethical monotheism that requires an unprecedented sense of moral responsibility toward one's fellow beings, demanding that we be our "brother's keeper."

God Is Perfect in His Goodness. Not having bodily form, God is not subject to human frailties and concessions to the flesh. God does not have to aspire to perfection. He has created the good and is its essence. He is the sum total of all human ideals extended to perfection. Men and women are able to conceive of love, truth, and justice because of God, who is perfect Love, perfect Truth, and perfect Justice. All the good that people do is attributed to God's influence in their lives.

God Is Omnipresent. He is not bound by spatial limitations or limitations of time. This attribute allows His presence to inhabit the entire universe, personally manifesting His influence everywhere simultaneously.

God and Man Are Copartners. God desires that each person cooperate in all worthwhile endeavors. Even though God is absolute, His influence can be felt only if the individual meets Him part of the way. In praying for peace, we cannot expect God to "take over" and establish or bring about the desired condition without our corresponding determination to work for peace. Humans are not helpless creatures who must sit and wait for God's grace. In Judaism people play an active role in their own redemption and the redemption of the world by helping to perfect the creation that God has intentionally left incomplete.

God Is Personal. There is a difference between depicting God as a person and claiming that He is personal. God is more than a mere Idea or Force–a creation of the human mind. He reacts to prayers. He deals with people singly and is aware of their individual needs and problems.

God Is Both Part of Humans and Independent of Them. He does not rely on humans for His existence, and yet part of God may be found in humans. It is the soul that God has implanted within us that makes it possible to speak of ourselves as created in God's image. Because of this soul, we can communicate with God. We can also learn God's qualities such as patience and compassion and thus we are able to imitate these divine characteristics.

In reading the Bible or prayer book we find many references to God in human terms. He is Father and King. He speaks, or walks, or stretches forth His hand. Such references are not to be taken literally, however, for the Bible speaks in the language of people so that the most simple among them will be aware of God's reality. It is impossible for finite minds to avoid pictorialization of an infinite being. We do not possess the celestial vocabulary to address God properly. If we did, we would be able to conceive of God's real essence. As long as we are aware that God is not corporeal and that we are symbolizing Him in saying "Thou" and "He," then we are not unjustified in our use of human descriptions.

As humankind continues to evolve spiritually and mentally, we may come to know more and more about God, just as our conception of Him has matured over the past centuries. His true essence, however, will forever be enshrouded in mystery.

Such knowledge is too wonderful for me,
Too high, I cannot attain to it.

"TELL ME ABOUT GOD"

Every parent is confronted at some time or other with questions about God. Whether or not His name is mentioned in the home, the child comes to wonder about the big world in which he or she lives. Who made the sky, the trees, and people? This sense of wonder extends to God. The child wants to know if he or she can see God or talk to Him.

The parent should not lose sight of the fact that children begin to formulate a readiness to conceive God long before their outward expressions of wonderment. The love that they receive from the cradle, the qualities of kindness and consideration that they experience, can in a way prepare them to accept the idea of a kind, considerate, and loving God. If, however, they are denied love in infancy, they may find God hard to accept. It is imperative, therefore, that infants see reflected in their parents those kindly, loving qualities that they can later identify with God.

There is great satisfaction in knowing that we are helping to provide a foundation that will enable the child to build an edifice of faith which can withstand the storms of denial and doubt. "Train the child in the way he should go, and when he is old he will not depart from it."

Q. "Who is God?"

A.   No one knows everything about God, not even the wisest person in the world. But the wiser we become, the more we learn about Him and His wonderful ways. God is the creator who formed our magnificent world. But He is

12

even more. To me, He is like an Unseen Friend who whispers into our ear and tells us the right thing to do. God wants us to do what He knows to be right, for He is all-good and knows more than anyone about right and wrong.

Q. "How does God speak to me?"

A. We do not hear a human voice when God speaks to us. God talks to us through a feeling that we get inside or an idea that comes to us. That is His way of speaking without words. God is speaking to us when He encourages us to be thoughtful and helpful. He is speaking to us when we make a wise decision or show that we are brave in time of danger. We can almost hear a voice inside saying, "I knew you would do it!"

Q. "What happens when we do not listen to Him?"

A. God will not make us listen to Him. He merely advises us, and the choice is up to us. When we refuse to listen to Him, then God cannot be responsible for what may happen to us. We really hurt ourselves.

Q. "Does God cause people to get sick?"

A. God does not cause sickness. Since God did not finish the creation of the world, He has left many things to be improved upon, such as our health, and has given us the wisdom to finish what He has left incomplete. We hope that someday all illness may be conquered by men and women, with God's help.

We do not know why good people suffer. But this we do know: sickness and pain are not always tragic. Sickness has often given people extraordinary courage and determination in their fight to get well. Their struggle against illness has often brought out their best qualities. They have learned to appreciate the beauty of life and the world about them. They have felt deeper sympathy for others in poor health.

Q.   *"Does God know everything I do?"*

A.   Yes. In addition to being all-good, God is all-knowing. Everything that we do or think or say is of interest to Him. People will often do evil things because they think that no one is watching them, but they cannot keep secrets from God, who is always in our presence.

Q.   *"Is God like a man?"*

A.   God is not like a man or any living being. He is different from all people in that He has no body or form. We could not exist long without food and shelter or the help of other people, but God is not dependent on other things or people for His existence.

Q. *"Why do we speak of God as Father?"*

A. Often we describe an unknown thing or idea by comparing it to something that is familiar to us. Not being able to describe God properly, we poetically speak of Him in terms of the best qualities that we know in such an esteemed person as our father, who loves and protects us. That does not mean that we believe God to be a person such as our father. The language of religion is a language of poetry.

Q. *"Does God live in the sky?"*

A. When we look at the sky, it is natural to think of God, for just as the sky is far above us, so is God higher and greater than ourselves. Both cause us to look up. But God is not only in the sky; He is everywhere. He is right before us and He is also across the ocean. He is in every city and every town.

Q. *"If I can't see God, how do I know He exists?"*

A. There are many things that exist even though we do not see them. Nobody has ever seen electricity, and yet we know it exists. We know what it does. It brings us light and heat; it causes machines to run and automobiles to travel. In other words, we come to know that electricity exists because we see what it does. In the same way, we do believe that God exists when we see people who are good and kind. God has influenced them to be that way.

Q.   *"Did God make the world?"* *

A.   Yes, God made the world and everything in it, but not at once. First He made the beautiful world that we live in, then He made the sky. God provided the world with trees, grass, and flowers; but these could not grow without the help of sunlight, so God decided to make His great helper, the sun, to make things grow and also to give us daylight. He also made the moon to give light by night.

But life would have been very dull without living things, so God made the fish to move around in the water, birds to fill the sky, and animals to roam the earth.

But God was still not satisfied, because He wanted someone to be His partner, someone who could think and make things too. So He created man, and then woman. With the woman by his side, man would not be lonely. He would have someone to speak with and someone to love.

---

* Note to Parents: Telling the story of creation can serve a twofold purpose: first, introducing the child to the Bible; second, teaching a functional concept of God, a concept growing out of the things that God does. A child thinks largely in terms of action–a chair is something to *sit* on, mother is someone who *cares* for you. Robbie Trent, in *Your Child and God*, (Chicago: Willett, Clark and Co.) makes the following observation: "God is related to the child's daily experiences. Out of the experiences, the things of which he is a part, he must build his concept of God."

Q.   "But how can you say that God made everything? I saw men building a house down the street."

A.   Remember that God made man because He wanted a partner to help Him create. You know where the wood comes from, don't you? Well, God wanted some of the trees to be used for houses, and He gave His partner a wonderful mind to be able to make a house from a tree.

God puts wonderful things in the world and helps us learn how to make the best use of them. He will not do things that people can do themselves because we would become lazy and expect God to do everything for us. People's talent would also go to waste. It is only when we can put those talents to use, such as the ability to make a house, that we can appreciate God's wonderful gifts.

Q.   "Can I talk to God?"

A.   Yes, you can talk to God and in any language, for God understands all languages. We call talking to God "prayer." God wants to hear us speak to Him because that is how we get to feel closer to Him, just as we feel closer to a friend with whom we speak regularly. He also wants to hear us pray, because our prayers make us think about wonderful things, such as improving ourselves and helping others.

Q.   *"What can I talk to God about?"*

A.   We can talk to God about many things. We can tell Him how thankful we are for His many gifts, such as the food we eat, our loving parents, our teachers. We thank Him for our rest at night, for the beautiful holidays He has given us to enjoy, for teaching us how to be good.

We can also ask God for important things, such as good health for ourselves, our family, and friends. When asking God for things, we do not expect Him to do tricks for us, such as changing a nickel into a dollar, nor do we ask Him for the less important things, such as helping our team win. We cannot expect God to serve everybody's personal wish, for He is interested in our requests only when they are important to others as well as to ourselves. Actually, prayer makes us think on the highest level that we know how. We think about improving ourselves, about helping others, about helping to make a better community and a better world in which to live.

Q.   *"What is the most important prayer in the Jewish prayer book?"*

A.   The oldest and most important prayer that Jews recite is the *Shema.* It is so old that it is found in the Bible. Observing Jews recite it every morning and evening and before retiring at night.

It is so important to the Jewish people because the main ideas of Judaism are found in the prayer. First, it stresses the oneness of God, probably the most important idea that the Jew gave the world. Belief in monotheism means that there is one God alone, and all people should show love and respect to the one God and to no being besides Him. Second, the *Shema* speaks of Israel's love for God and His commandments. As Jews we agree to remain faithful to God forever by thinking about Him, by teaching about Him, and by following those ceremonies that remind us of Him.

Q. *"Can I pray anywhere?"*

A. Yes, you can pray to God anywhere and at any time. Since God is not limited to any one place, He receives our sincere prayers wherever they may be offered. Some people are moved to pray outdoors when they are surrounded by the beauty of nature, other wish to pray in a hospital room where a sick person is confined to bed. There are many prayers that are to be said in the home and others said in the synagogue.

Just because God accepts our prayers in all places does not mean that it is unnecessary to pray in the synagogue. There are times, such as the Sabbath and holidays, when public worship is very important. On these days it is a religious duty to hear the Torah* reading, which should be done in public. When praying in the synagogue, we also feel a sense of kinship with the other worshipers who are reciting the same prayers. The rabbi's sermon, the synagogue music, and the beautiful atmosphere in which we worship all help to put us in a mood for prayer.

---

* *Torah* consists of the five books of Moses. A portion of the Torah is read in the synagogue every Sabbath and holiday. The Torah scroll, which is written by hand, is the most sacred object of the Jewish people.

Q.　"*Why must I recite someone else's prayers instead of my own?*"

A.　Judaism does encourage private prayer. In fact, a person who reads only the prayers in the *Siddur* (prayer book) is not fulfilling his or her religious duty. However, the prayers that appear in the *Siddur* represents a collection of the finest thoughts of many great men down through the ages, and we might not be able to write or deliver prayers as fine. Therefore, we use their wonderful words to help us express our own thoughts. In this way also we feel a sense of oneness with all our brothers and sisters in the present and past who have ever recited these prayers in Hebrew.

THE HEBREW BIBLE
"WHAT'S IN THE BIBLE?"

Chapter II

THE HEBREW BIBLE

The Hebrew Bible or *TaNaKH* relates the struggles of the Jewish people in search of their God. It records their frustrations, doubts, and reversals along with their progress, hopes, and fulfillments. It is a running commentary on life as it was lived, with no details ignored. It is neither squeamish in discussing immorality nor sparing in praise for the righteous, interpreting both extremes as part of life's story.

No type of person is neglected in the Bible: the wise and the foolish, the poor and the prosperous, the kind and the wicked, the pragmatist and the dreamer make up the cast of characters. All may be found within the pages of the book that has captured the imagination of young and old alike for centuries and has served to remind readers of the basic sameness of human nature.

The name "Bible" comes from the Greek *biblos*, which means "book." In reality, the Bible is a library of many books, written at different times by different authors in different lands, and in many literary forms, including poetry, drama, biography, and exalted prose.

The word *TaNaKH* is made up of three Hebrew initials representing the divisions of the Bible. T –*Torah*, N –*Neviim* or "Prophets," and KH –Ketuvim or "Writings." The *Torah* comprises the Five Books of Moses, which tell of the origin of the universe, the human race, primeval nations, and the people of Israel. The Exodus from Egypt, leading to God's revelation of the *Torah* at Mt. Sinai, climaxes this first part of the Bible. After the revelation, most of the remaining pages deal with the various laws that the Israelites were to adopt upon entering the land of Canaan. Rules for social, ritual, and moral guidance are included in this blueprint of Israel's future way of life upon settlement in the land.

The section called *Neviim* or "Prophets" includes the books of Isaiah, Jeremiah, Ezekiel and the Twelve from Hosea to Malachi. It commences with the book of Joshua, followed by the era when the Judges ruled Israel; it then traces the history of Israel's monarchy, beginning with Saul, and concludes with the return from Babylonian exile. Most important, however, this section deals extensively with the teachings of the great prophets of Israel, who brought the word of God to a wandering and often erring people. These prophets, driven against their will to speak to the people, and incurring the scorn and punishment of the ruling classes, were swept by a force greater than themselves to defy convention and to sacrifice worldly comforts for the sake of righteousness.

The *Ketuvim* or "Writings" include the Psalms, which are prayers composed over a period of centuries; Proverbs, a collection of sayings dealing with proper conduct; Job, dealing with the problem of God's justice; Ecclesiastes; Lamentations; the Song of Songs; and the historical books of Ruth, Esther, Daniel, Ezra, Nehemiah, and Chronicles.

In each of the Bible's three sections, Jewish history is blended with religion and morality. Despite obvious differences in form and presentation, a spirit of unity pervades all the books of the Bible. God is revealing Himself to humans and making His will known to them.

The ancients knew nothing of modern distinctions between religion and science. That explains why one finds in the Bible "scientific" observations which were acceptable in their day. Many moderns who are troubled by the Bible because they cannot accept its outmoded scientific data fail to realize that its authors were not basically concerned with facts but rather with truths, eternal verities. They wanted to tell how God expects people to live in the world that he created for them.

True, the Biblical authors were curious about many of the phenomena with which modern science has dealt. They wondered about the origin of the world, the beginning of arts and crafts, and the different languages of mankind. They were concerned with the mysteries of nature—the rainbow in the storm clouds, the flood, and the earthquake. However, to them, all of nature's wonders were considered to be God's way of teaching great spiritual lessons. For instance, the appearance of the rainbow meant that God would not destroy the world again as He did in the time of Noah. The rainbow came to be associated with the spirit of faith and optimism. Similarly, the author was curious to know about the origin of the "pillars of salt" near the south end of the Dead Sea. They were actually formed as pieces of salt became detached by the rains, but he associated them with Lot's escape from Sodom: Lot's wife looked back at the demolished city and was transformed into salt. Clearly, the lesson is intended to teach that one should not look back with remorse for having left a place of iniquity.

Despite the fact that the Bible is not a book of science, it is interesting to note that archaeological studies have substantiated most of the historical places and many of the incidents mentioned in the Bible. Many of the minerals that were said to be used in Solomon's time, for instance, have been discovered in modern Israel. In fact, the Bible has been of inestimable value in helping to locate and exploit certain natural resources.

Likewise, the Bible has shed much light on certain historical periods that might otherwise have remained obscure to this day. Life in Palestine eight centuries before the Common Era can be reconstructed by reading the four prophets who lived and preached at that time. The social and religious customs as well as the political and economic conditions are clearly defined in the books of Amos, Hosea, Isaiah, and Micah. In addition, the Book of Esther has been of great help to students of ancient Persian history, presenting a vivid picture of life in the Persian court and royal harem which is not found in other sources of information.

The books that were included in the Holy Scriptures constitute what is called "Canon." The Bible was canonized in the second century before the Common Era, although controversies about certain books continued for many years afterward.

There are many religious books that were excluded when the Bible was put into final form. They are known as *Apocrypha*, which in Greek means "hidden," because they were prohibited for sacred use and were not permitted to be kept with the other religious books but instead were placed in a store room for private reading. It is not known exactly why some of these books were excluded from the Canon but it is believed that they lacked the religious intensity of the canonical books, or perhaps they did not have the necessary nationalistic appeal. Among these semi-sacred works are the books of the Maccabees, Judith, Tobit and the Wisdom of Ben Sira.

The Christian Bible consists of our *TaNaKH* (which Christians call the Old Testament) plus the New Testament. Jews do not generally speak of the Bible as the Old Testament since they cannot accept the Christian belief that the Old Testament was merely a prelude to the climactic event of world history—namely, the birth, life, and death of Jesus. In the

Christian view, the New Testament represents a higher development of religious thought. Since Jews do not accept this idea, they do not use the terminology that supports it.

The earliest translation of the Bible was into Greek about 300 years before the Common Era. It was called Septuagint, which means "seventy," referring to the legend that the translation was composed by seventy Jews. The Bible was translated into Greek so that the Jews living in Greek-speaking countries could understand it. The Vulgate, a Latin translation of the Bible by one of the leaders of the early Christian Church, Jerome, appeared in the fifth century. Having studied with Jewish teachers in Palestine, Jerome was well qualified to undertake the task of translation.

For Jews the English translation issued by the Jewish Publication Society has been considered the most authentic. A group of American Jewish scholars worked on that translation for about ten years before it was published in 1917. As its preface indicates, they aimed to combine the spirit of Jewish tradition with the results of Biblical scholarship. The need for this translation by Jewish scholars grew out of a feeling that "the Jew cannot afford to have his Bible translation prepared for him by others . . . even as he cannot borrow his soul from others." In the 1980's a new translation of the Holy Scriptures appeared.

Hundreds of book have been written about the influence of the Bible on world thought. Its spirit pervades our greatest documents such as the Magna Charta, the Declaration of Independence, and the Constitution of the United States. Setting forth the underlying principles of freedom and democracy, the Bible is an indispensable source book for the understanding of our American heritage.

The world's greatest literary artists have been influenced by Biblical thinking. As Nicholas Murray Butler said on one occasion: "Without the Bible it is impossible to understand the literature of the English language from Chaucer to Browning." Without the Bible there would have been no *Paradise Lost*, no *Pilgrim's Progress*. Shakespeare was well acquainted with Biblical thought and style, using Biblical terms and allusions with great ease. Tennyson's works were saturated with Biblical content. James Russell Lowell, Henry Wordsworth Longfellow, and John Greenleaf Whittier were all greatly influenced by the Bible. Matthew Arnold made the Bible his constant companion.

Many American presidents were also assiduous students of the Book. Lincoln mastered the Bible, adopting its language and style in his speeches and writings. Distinctive echoes of Biblical phraseology resound throughout his Gettysburg Address and Emancipation Proclamation.

Even though the Bible has become the common possession of the entire western world, it has a special claim for reverence among Jews. The authors of the Bible and almost all its personalities are Jews. Its messages of warning and hope are addressed to Israel. The relationship between the people of Israel and the land of Israel pervades throughout. Furthermore, the Bible stresses the unique covenant that existed between God and Israel. "You are My witnesses," "You shall be unto Me a Kingdom of priests and a holy nation," "You shall be holy unto Me."

Because the *Torah* represented the revealed word of God and was a major part of Judaism, Jews studied it assiduously and taught it diligently to their children. The practice of reading a portion of the *Torah* and selections from the prophets in the synagogue every Sabbath was instituted in Talmudic times in order to complete the reading of the entire *Torah* along with selected prophetic passages within the year.

It was not considered sufficient for Jews merely to read the *Torah*, but it was necessary also to study it and the various commentaries to understand better the intent of its passages and the meaning behind many of its more cryptic statements. In Eastern Europe a boy at seven had already begun to acquaint himself with the difficult Rashi script and commentary.

The *Torah* was intensively studied not only because of its inherent value as the revealed word but also because it was the key to the understanding of all Jewish law and literature. Whether one was grappling with a legal passage in the Talmud, studying Jewish lore, reading a Hebrew poem, or reciting the daily prayers, the *Torah* was the key to all these.

Because the *Torah* was so basic to the understanding of all Jewish literature, the word's meaning was eventually expanded to include everything that had its roots in the *Torah* —the entire Jewish culture from Mosaic to modern times. To study *Torah* meant to delve into any book written in the spirit of the original, whether it was rabbinic literature, Biblical commentaries, or Jewish philosophy. *Torah* study was accorded the highest place in Judaism. Its importance was equated with the fulfillment of all the commandments of Judaism. No Jew could aspire to the Jewish ideal without constant study, which was the very condition of survival and salvation.

"WHAT'S IN THE BIBLE?"

The Bible can serve as a most effective introduction to the child's understanding of moral issues. In addition, it gives the parent abundant material from which to choose stories, sayings, and parables based on ethical themes.

Reading the Bible aloud can be of great value to young children even though they may not understand all that is read to them. It serves a useful purpose even if they learn only to familiarize themselves with names and places, and with its beauty and majesty of language.

The Bible lends itself to so much interrogation that people of all ages have never ceased discussing it. It is interesting to observe that many of the questions that children ask about the Bible are similar to the problems that have interested the most astute scholars. For instance, both the seven-year-old and the serious Biblical student are interested in knowing why God prohibited Adam from eating the fruit from the Tree of Knowledge.

The answers that we offer our children must, of necessity, be only partial. It is impossible to know exactly what the author was thinking and the exact context in which he wrote. Only the keenest scholar is able to probe the Biblical mind and understand its total universe of discourse.

It is wise from the very outset to indicate to the inquisitive child that the Bible was not intended to teach us lessons in science—today we have modern science books for that—but as a guide for living the good life, nothing can compare to the Bible in greatness.

Q. *"Must we believe everything that the Bible says to be factual?"* *

A. No, it is not the factual information that makes the Bible so great but rather its eternal truths. For instance, that God really created one man by the name of Adam before all other people were created is probably not fact. The truth that the Bible wants to impress us with is that since Adam and Eve were the parents of the human race, all their descendants are brothers and sisters.

People often spend too much time discussing whether certain events could really have taken place. They are more interested in proving or disproving the Bible from a scientific view than they are in understanding its moral teachings. Rather than merely stating a set of ethical rules for us, the Bible teaches the difference between right and wrong through interesting events and beautiful tales.

---

* Note to Parents: The basic difference between the Orthodox and modernist viewpoint rests on the answer to this question. The Orthodox Jew believes that the whole *Torah* was revealed by God at Sinai, while the modernist believes the *Torah* to have been written by inspired men at different times.

Q. *"Why did God create Adam and Eve?"*

A. After God created the animals, He was still not completely satisfied. He wanted a creature that would be made in His image, that is, with a mind to know the difference between right and wrong, which the animals did not have.

God also wanted someone to help Him make the world a good place in which to live by making the most of his abilities, by creating new and wonderful things.

God also wanted His creation to have the intelligence to understand that there is a God, which even the highest form of animal could never imagine. If the first man and woman could but think of God, perhaps they would want to follow His ways. So He formed Adam and Eve, His greatest creation.

Q.   *"Do the names Adam and Eve have any meaning in Hebrew?"*

A.   Yes, all Hebrew names have a symbolic meaning. "Adam" is derived from the Hebrew *adamah*, meaning "earth," from which the first man was said to have been created. Adam's wife was called *Havah* or "Eve," which means "living," because all human life came from her.

Q.   *"Can we believe in evolution and still accept the Bible?"*

A.   The author of Genesis may have sensed that the higher forms, such as humans, came from the lower forms of life, and that is why man is described as the climax of God's creation, following after plant life, and the sea and land animals.

Certainly the author could not have been acquainted with the scientific explanation of evolution. His main purpose in writing about creation was to explain not the origin of the human race but rather its spiritual kinship with God: "And God created man in His image; in the image of God did He create him."

Belief in the theory of evolution should not at all weaken our faith in God. In fact, when we believe that the development of humans from the lower forms of life has not been accidental but rather the result of purpose and design, then evolution can have great religious meaning for us: we can see how wonderful are the ways of God in having created a fully developed person with a mind and soul.

Q. *"If God wanted man to become wise, why did He not want Adam and Eve to eat from the Tree of Knowledge?"*

A. As was mentioned above, this question has attracted the attention of countless Biblical students. Perhaps God would have given Adam this knowledge eventually, for that is why man was created. But He wanted Adam to obey Him first, which was even more important than the possession of knowledge. When Eve was told by the serpent that she and Adam would be like God and know everything, they could not resist taking the fruit. It was Adam's and Eve's disobedience that caused them to be punished.

Q. *"Did Methuselah really live 969 years?"*

A. Undoubtedly Methuselah and other men who lived before Noah did not live as long as the Bible says they did. The reason some of the men in the Bible were described as having lived so long stems from the influence of the neighboring cultures upon the Hebrews. When we read some of the Babylonian stories about their godlike kings who lived tens of thousands of years, we can understand how hard it was to wipe out the notion among the ancient Hebrews that their heroes were likewise divine. By the way of compromise, the Bible described men such as Methusaleh as having lived less than a thousand years, which the Bible speaks of as the length of one full divine day. Thus men like Methuselah were pictured as mortals and not gods.

Q.   *"How did the Jewish people come to be?"*

A.   When Abraham left his birthplace in the Euphrates Valley so that he could worship the one God that he had discovered, he settled in the desert and became the head of a large clan of wandering shepherds called Hebrews. They traveled from one green spot to another until the grass was gone. But their destination was Canaan, "the land that I will show you." It was Abraham who was the father of the Hebrew people, who were the first to believe in one God, and with whom God made a special treaty or covenant. After the death of Abraham, his son Isaac took his place as leader of the Hebrews, and after Isaac came Jacob, the grandson of Abraham. God changed Jacob's name to Israel, and his followers, bearing his name, called themselves the Children of Israel, or Israelites.

Q.   *"Why did Abraham and Jacob each have two wives?"*

A.   It was not considered sinful to have more than one wife in Bible times, but even then there was a trend toward monogamy (marriage to one wife). Abraham's wife Sarah did not give birth to Isaac until her old age. Abraham took a second wife, Hagar, into his home to bear him a child, not knowing that Sarah would eventually have one herself. He felt that he had to fulfill the promise that God had made him, namely, that his descendants would be as numerous as the stars in the heavens.

Isaac had only one wife, Rebecca.

Jacob wanted Rachel as his only wife but was deceived by Laban into taking Leah, Rachel's older sister. He was then permitted to marry Rachel if he agreed to serve Laban for another seven years.

Q. *"Why do Jews revere Moses?"*

A. Moses could probably have become a great Egyptian leader since he was brought up in the Pharaoh's palace, but he chose instead to cast his lot with the suffering people of Israel, knowing very well that he would be considered an enemy of the Pharaoh. It was Moses who freed the Hebrew slaves and unified them into a people with a common belief and a common purpose. It was Moses who gave them God's law to live by. For these reasons he was considered the greatest of Israel's prophets.

Q. *"What is the Burning Bush?"*

A. It was at the Burning Bush that God appeared to Moses and made His true name known. No one before or after Moses had come so close to God as did Moses at the Burning Bush.

The vision of Moses became a symbol of the Jewish people throughout the ages. They have been oppressed time and again and yet, like the Burning Bush that was not consumed, they have never been destroyed.

Q. "*Why could Moses not enter the Promised Land, especially if he was so righteous?*"

A.   According to tradition, Moses was not permitted to enter the land of Israel because he lost his temper and smote the rock instead of following God's command of speaking to it to bring forth water. We are told that because he was so great he should have set an example by restraining himself.

Like Moses, people often give their lives over to a cause and yet they do not live to see the completion of their work. President Roosevelt was largely responsible for the United Nations and yet did not live to see the opening of that great organization. Theodor Herzl gave his life to Zionism and died before Israel became a Jewish state.

Q.   "*Why are the Ten Commandments so important?*"

A.   The Ten Commandments are a set of rules which are the minimum requirements of life for Jews as well as all people in our society. There are, of course, many other laws not included in the Ten Commandments which are necessary if we are to live a complete Jewish life, just as a citizen of the United States is expected to do more than merely follow the Constitution in order to be considered a good citizen.

Q.   "Is not the Biblical law about 'an eye for an eye' very harsh?"

A.   The intention of the Bible in setting down the law about "an eye for an eye" was to teach that a person should not suffer greater damage than he or she caused.

There are some scholars who have shown that even at the time when the law was written in the Bible, it did not mean that the guilty man's eye should be taken out because he had put out someone else's eye, but rather that he should pay the victim the value of the eye. Limbs were evaluated then, as they are by insurance companies today.

Q.   "What does the Bible say about the dietary laws?"

A.   The Bible does not go into great detail about the dietary laws. It merely states that one should not seethe a kid in its mother's milk. The animals that may and may not be eaten are mentioned. The prohibitions against eating blood and tearing off the limb of a live animal are also included. Most of the details regarding *kashrut* were formed after the Bible was written.

Q.   "Were the prophets really able to look into the future?"

A.   Often the prophets would predict the results of sin, or they would tell of the enemy that would overtake Israel or Judah in the future, but they were not soothsayers or fortune-tellers. They had remarkable insight and could predict the course of future events on the basis of present conditions.

They knew that punishment at the hand of God would result from the sins of the people.

However, this was not the main function of the prophet. The Hebrew word for prophet, *Navi*, means "spokesman." He was a spokesman for God, a man who, often against his will, was delegated to bring God's word to the people. Usually he would tell them about things they wanted least to hear–their own wrongdoings.

Q.   "If the Christian accepts the Old Testament, why can't we accept the New Testament?"

A.   Christians accept the Old Testament as an introduction to the New. They say that the New Testament is a fulfillment of the Old, and they attempt to show that the prophets predicted the coming of Jesus.

Jews, on the other hand, accept only the Old Testament, which we refer to as the Hebrew Bible, because we believe that it is complete in itself rather than an introduction to something greater. Interpretations of the Hebrew Bible such as the Talmud explain in detail many of the Biblical laws, but they do no supersede the Bible. They only help to strengthen it.

Furthermore, we do not agree that Jesus was divine and that the miracles related about him in the New Testament are authentic. The crucifixion and resurrection represent the nucleus of the New Testament, around which everything else revolves.

Q.   *"May Jews read the New Testament?"*

A.   Yes. It helps us understand the Jewish history of the early Christian era. We find it interesting to compare the New Testament and Hebrew Bible and to see how passages such as the Sermon on the Mount follow closely the form and content of the Hebrew Bible.

❖*Chapter III*

RELIGIOUS DUTIES AND PRACTICES OF THE JEW
"WHAT DO THESE CUSTOMS MEAN?"

Chapter III

RELIGIOUS DUTIES AND PRACTICES OF THE JEW

Many of the religious ideals that Judaism set forth centuries ago have now become the common possession of other major faiths. Its customs and practices, however, have remained unique to the Jewish people and were not adopted by the founders of any other groups. For instance, the Gentiles who were converted to Christianity sought to distinguish themselves from the Jews by adopting Sunday as their Sabbath; Mohammed instituted Friday as the Moslem Sabbath.

Jews, however, despite every conceivable pressure, clung to their rituals with a fervor that defied persuasion, coercion, and even physical torture. Though a Jew might permit himself the luxury of differing from his fellow Jews about the doctrines and beliefs of Judaism, he never allowed himself to deviate from the rituals and disciplines that were imposed upon him. The *mitzvah* or "commandment" was divinely ordained and could not be reinterpreted to suit whim or convenience. The traditional Jew was also aware that the meticulous observance of these *mitzvot* preserved one's national existence and assured Jewish survival. He took issue with those Jews who arbitrarily accepted certain laws and rejected others. "Once you begin to make changes," he would say,

43

"you will end up without anything." Jewish life would then be subject to extinction, unable to preserve itself against the alien currents of the outside world.

As a result of such apprehensions, the religious authorities added new *mitzvot* to the old in order to make a "fence around the Torah." The rationale was that if the principal observances of Judaism were endangered, then new barriers in the form of additional ceremonial practices should be set up as a protection.

Though the personal observance of Jewish ritual has been on the decline in modern times, there is still a general adherence to certain public ceremonies that highlight the lifetime of the Jew. These are as follows:

The circumcision of male children on the eighth day, signifying the *Brit* or *"covenant"* between God and Israel.

The naming of newly born girls in the synagogue and boys at the *Brit*.

The *Pidyon Haben* or "Redemption of the first-born son" from the *Kohen*, who technically releases the first child and returns him to the possession of the parents.

The *Bar Mitzvah* ceremony, which signifies that the Jewish male adolescent is prepared to assume the obligations of Jewish life.

The *Bat Mitzvah* ceremony, in which the Jewish girl undergoes the same experience, and which has recently become a major ceremony in Jewish life.

The calling of the groom to the *Torah* on the Sabbath before his marriage.

The wedding ceremony, with its canopy under which the bride and groom stand side by side, the transfer of the ring to consummate the marriage, and the glass which is broken by the groom.

In bereavement, the rituals that attend the funeral and interment: the *shivah* period observed by the mourners; the recitation of *Kaddish* for eleven months in the synagogue signifying the mourner's acceptance of God's will even in time of anguish; the unveiling of the tombstone toward the end of the year; the observance of *yahrzeit* by lighting a twenty-four-hour candle and reciting the *Kaddish*; the observance of *Yizkor* on *Yom Kippur* and on the three major festivals.

In addition to these ceremonies which still maintain a strong hold on a large segment of American Jews, even many of those who have veered away from personal observance, there also exists a deep abiding reverence for ceremonial objects used in the synagogue and home—the prayer book, the *Kiddush* cup, the *mezuzah*, the *menorah*.

For what reasons were the rituals given to Israel anyway? Neither the *Torah* nor the Talmud gives the reasons for most of the *mitzvot*. But the traditionalist, because of a firm belief in revelation, did not need reasons for observing the laws. "God enacted a decree and I am not at liberty to deviate from it," he would say. When Maimonides, medieval Jewry's most outstanding scholar, attempted to find reasons for the various laws in his *Guide for the Perplexed*, he was severely criticized by his contemporaries. "If the reason that you give becomes obsolete, then people will cease to observe the Law," they said.

And yet, because the modern mind demands understanding, reasons for the observance of ritual may be listed as follows:

1. The *sanctification of natural human drives*. Judaism believes that since these drives are God-given, they should not be frustrated. Scores of rituals center around the eating of food—the

washing of hands, the various blessings, the grace after meals. The recitation of *Kiddush* over wine falls into this same general category. Jews are not bidden to refrain from wine but rather to sanctify their natural God-given desire for indulgence by pronouncing a blessing over it. In fact, the Nazarite who vowed not to drink strong drink had to bring a special offering before the Lord because he willfully denied himself one of the pleasures of life. The wedding ceremony, too, is intended to elevate one's biological desire so that it becomes sanctioned by a sacred ceremony. (In fact, the Hebrew word for marriage is *kiddushin,* which means "holiness.")

2. *The necessity of moderation and discipline.* Natural human desires, if carried to an extreme, could serve evil consequences. It is a *mitzvah* to eat, but not excessively. Likewise, we are exhorted to drink, but not to a point of intoxication.

The dietary laws are intended not only to teach moderation in our diet, but to influence us to practice sobriety in everything that we do. Unlike the animals, humans can control their appetites, and one of the purposes of ritual is to help them learn how to resist.

People must train themselves systematically in discipline. Just as the musician or athlete must abide by regulations and schedules to succeed, so must all mortals be bound by self-control to attain their spiritual goals.

That is why Judaism lays great emphasis on performing commandments within stipulated time schedules, and why precision and care are stressed in the fulfillment of *mitzvot.* For instance, prayers are to be recited within certain specified hours; the Sabbath is ushered in twenty minutes before sunset and bidden farewell with the appearance of three stars in the heaven.

3. *The educational value of ritual.* The various Jewish rituals and ceremonies serve the purpose of inculcating ideas dramatically through audio-visual means. For example, Passover basically concerns itself with the ideal of freedom. The entire *seder* ceremony serves to impress on the mind of the participant this theme of freedom. The matzah, the bitter herbs, the four cups of wine, the roasted egg–all these are visual symbols

intended to create an indelible impression upon the participant. Since memory is an essential aspect of education, Judaism tends to create feelings of nostalgia in persons who have at one time participated in the Jewish ceremonials. Jewish literature is replete with the experiences of so-called renegades who eventually return to Judaism after years of abstinence through a yearning desire to be with their people on a *seder* night or at a *Kol Nidre* service.

The observance of rituals also serves to help us formulate and maintain ethical standards. They remind us constantly that it is our task to lead moral lives. Our rabbis put it succinctly in the Talmud: "The *mitzvot* were given primarily to refine human nature."

4. *A sense of group solidarity.* All historic rituals help to unite us in time and in space with our fellow Jews throughout the world. The recitation of prayers in the original Hebrew helps to remind us that our forebears communicated with God in the same language. We feel that we are helping to contribute toward the survival of Judaism by observing the same rituals that are being followed by Jews throughout the world.

Similarly, a greater feeling of unity and strength is experienced within a community when its members engage in prayer or ritual acts together. Differences are often minimized; common interests and aspirations are emphasized.

5. *Strengthening of family bonds.* Most Jewish rituals center around the home rather than the synagogue. In an age when the home is losing importance, Jewish ceremonies help to unite the family, giving each member of the household a distinct function to fulfill. Many students of sociology have agreed that the remarkable history of Jewish family solidarity has been due largely to the emphasis on home rituals involving every member.

The following prayer, which is part of the meditation before the kindling of Sabbath lights, emphasizes this point:

Father of Mercy, O continue Your lovingkindness unto me and my dear ones. Make me worth to rear my children that they walk in the way of the righteous before You, loyal to Your Law and clinging to good deeds. Keep from us all manner of shame, grief, and care; and grant that peace, light, and joy ever abide in our home.

"WHAT DO THESE CUSTOMS MEAN?"

If the child is impressed with the relevance of rituals and their importance in daily living, then he or she will be eager to participate in them. Many ceremonies, however, can be appreciated and understood only after their completion. Trying to make the child understand their value before he experiences them is like teaching a child the value of reading before he has read his first book. The emotional and intellectual satisfaction comes only after the habit of reading has been created.

When the Israelites who stood at Sinai were asked to accept the Torah, *with which they were not yet acquainted, they nevertheless responded: "We shall do and we will understand." Our children can be taught to participate in Jewish ceremonials with the hope of appreciating their full value in the course of time.*

Ceremonies in the Lifetime of a Jew

Q. *"When is a boy or girl named?"*

A.   The boy is named on the eighth day after birth when he is circumcised. Girls are usually named in the synagogue soon after birth, at which time the father is called up to the *Torah* and the name is given.

Q. *"When do we use our Hebrew names?"*

A.   Our Hebrew names are used at any religious function, such as when being called up to the *Torah*.   Often children are called by their Hebrew names in religious

49

school. Also, when couples are married, the rabbi asks for their Hebrew names to be filled into the *ketubah*, or marriage contract. A Hebrew name makes us feel closer to the Jewish people, for whom Hebrew is sacred. Furthermore, we are able to continue the memory of our ancestor who was called by the same name.

Q.   "Why is the circumcision ceremony so important?"

A.   The *brit milah* or "circumcision" is the oldest religious ceremony in Judaism. It was observed by Abraham and his descendants as a covenant between God and Israel long before the *Torah* was given to Israel. This ceremony of initiation into the family of Israel is considered so important that it is not postponed even if the eighth day after birth falls on the Sabbath or *Yom Kippur*.

Q.   "Is there a special ceremony for the first born?"

A.   Yes. When the first-born child is a boy, traditional Jews celebrate a ritual called *Pidyon Haben,* or "redemption of the first born." On the thirty-first day after birth, family and friends gather to witness this ceremony in which the father stands before a *Kohen* or "priest" and "offers" him either his child or five silver dollars instead of his son. The *Kohen* takes the redemption money and blesses the child with the priestly blessing.

The ceremony of *Pidyon Haben* dates back to very ancient times when the first-born son was believed to belong to God. However, the tribe of Levi was set aside to act as priests and servants in the Temple in place of the first-born Israelite, who was freed from service by the payment of five shekels to the sanctuary. It is considered a ceremony of thanksgiving by the parents for the privilege of redeeming their son.

Q. *"Will I really become a man when I am* Bar Mitzvah?" *"Will I be called a woman after my* Bat Mitzvah?"

A. Only a few generations ago, a boy would begin to earn his living after he reached his thirteenth birthday, unless, of course, he continued his studies in the *Yeshiva*. He did in that sense become a man at *Bar Mitzvah*. Today, however, since we are still dependent on our parents at thirteen, we cannot really be considered men. But we do change in that we and not our parents become responsible for carrying out our religious duties. Also, we are invited to participate in the religious life of the synagogue for the first time.

We also don't become women on the occasion of our *Bat Mitzvah*. This ceremony is a very important step on the way to our becoming mature Jewish women. The Bat Mitzvah, however, does entitle us to participate with the adults in the congregation and to be given most of the religious privileges and responsibilities that are available to the adult community.

Q. *"What is the meaning of the* huppah?"

A. The *huppah* is a canopy, which is usually a piece of cloth held up by four poles. It has probably grown out of the medieval custom of covering the bride and groom with a *tallit* or prayer shawl. Today it has taken on another meaning: It symbolizes the home into which the bride and groom enter once they are married.

Q. "Why does the groom step on the glass at the end of the ceremony?"

A.   We do not know how this custom began, but there is an interesting clue to be found in the Talmud. A rabbi noticed at his son's wedding that some guests were disorderly during the ceremony. He took an expensive cup and broke it before them so that they would become more attentive.

Today the breaking of the glass reminds us that bride and groom should not forget the serious side of life even in the midst of their greatest happiness. Others say that the purpose of breaking the glass is to remind us of the destruction of the Temple by the Romans.

The Synagogue, Its Symbols and Rituals

Q.   "What is a synagogue?"

A.   Any place where people gather to pray and in which there is an ark and *Torah* is called a synagogue. Since ancient times, the synagogue has been used for three main purposes: it is known as a "house of prayer," where public worship is held; a "house of study," where children and adults learn about their culture and religion; and a "house of assembly," where Jews gather for social purposes.

Q.   "How can I tell the difference between an Orthodox, Conservative, and Reform synagogue?"

A.   In the Orthodox synagogue one finds that the men and women are separated during times of prayer, and that during worship the men wear hats and prayer shawls. The service is conducted almost entirely in Hebrew by the cantor, who faces the ark.

Conservative synagogues are not as uniform in practice as the Orthodox. For instance, in some we may find the use of instrumental music. However, most Conservative synagogues can be identified in the following ways: men and women are seated together, the men wearing hats and prayer shawls; the cantor faces the congregation when leading the service; the prayers are mostly in Hebrew, but some are recited in English.

A Reform synagogue may usually be identified in the following ways: the men pray without hats or prayer shawls; English is the main language of worship; instrumental music and mixed choirs are generally used; men and women are seated together.

Q.   "What are the duties of a rabbi?"

A.   Years ago the duties of a rabbi differed considerably from those of most rabbis of today. The rabbi was mainly a religious authority who was called upon to decide questions of ritual and to resolve legal and communal problems among Jews. He reserved ample time to continue his studies, the necessity of which was recognized by the community, who looked upon him as a symbol of scholarship and tradition. The modern rabbi, though primarily a student and teacher of

Judaism, is engaged in a greater variety of activities: delivering a weekly sermon and being called upon to address numerous groups that meet in and outside the synagogue; usually supervising the religious school and often teaching its children; conducting adult classes; officiating at religious functions; devoting a considerable amount of time to visiting the sick and bereaved, and sharing the problems of the congregation. The rabbi is considered a representative of the Jewish people and serves as their ambassador of good will in the general community.

Q. "Who can lead a religious service?"

A.   Anyone who knows the service may lead the congregation in prayer. However, most of the large congregations engage a *hazzan* or "cantor" to lead the main services. Possessing a musical background and trained voice, the cantor is able to interpret the prayers in a way that appeals to the ear and encourages greater devotion. The duties of the modern cantor often include the training of a choir, preparation of *Bar Mitzvah* candidates, and instruction in the school.

Q.   "What is the most important ritual object in the synagogue?"

A.   The Scroll of the Law or *Torah*, from which the portion of the week is read every Sabbath, is the most important object in the synagogue. The greatest amount of care must be given to the *Torah*, not only when it is in use but also when it is resting in the ark. Defects in the Scroll are repaired immediately; it is not considered proper to touch the parchment but rather one must use a pointer *(yad, meaning "hand")* when reading it. The *Torah* is often adorned with a crown and other beautiful ornaments. When it is carried around the synagogue, everyone is required to stand. Also, when the ark is open, the congregation rises as a sign of respect for the Law.

Q. *"What is an aliyah?"*

A. *Aliyah* really means "going up." It is an honor given to the worshiper to ascend the pulpit and recite the blessings over the *Torah*. It is this *aliyah* given to the *Bar Mitzvah* for the first time that symbolizes promotion to responsibility.

Eight men (in some synagogues, women as well), including the *maftir*, receive *aliyot* on Sabbath morning; seven on the Day of Atonement; six on the festivals; four on the New Moon; and three at all other services when the *Torah* is read. The first *aliyah* is given to a descendant of Aaron *(Kohen)*, if there is one in the synagogue. The second is to a Levite, and the others are called from the remainder of the congregation, the Israelites.

Q. *"Who is a* Kohen?"

A. A *Kohen* is a descendant of Aaron, the brother of Moses, who was the first high priest in Israel. In the days of the Holy Temple the priests performed the sacrifices and led the people in prayer. Today the *Kohen* enjoys certain privileges because of his honored background. He is the first to be called to the *Torah*, and he participates in the *Pidyon Haben* ceremony. His first-born son, however, is exempt from being redeemed. In the more traditional congregations he is given the honor of asking God's blessing upon the worshipers in the same way that the ancient priests recited the blessings before the congregation of Israel.

Usually a Jew whose last name is Cohen, Katz, or Kaplan is a *Kohen*, but he may have another family name and still be a descendant of Aaron.

Q.   "Who is a Levite?"

A.   The Levites in ancient days helped the priests in the Temple. They were also the singers and the keepers of the Temple gate. Today they are privileged to be called to the *Torah* immediately after the *Kohen*. As with the *Kohen*, the Levite's first-born son is not redeemed.

Usually a family bearing the name Levy, Levine, or Siegel is a descendant of the family of *Levi*. However, like the *Kohen*, the *Levi* cannot be determined by the family name alone.

Q.   "What is the Siddur?"

A.   The *Siddur* is a book containing the daily and Sabbath prayers recited in the home and synagogue. The most frequent prayers, comprising the daily service, are arranged in the beginning of the book. The Sabbath service is then introduced, followed by the prayers for the holidays. Thus the word *Siddur*, which means "order" or "arrangement."

Though individual prayers in the *Siddur* are thousands of

years old, the traditional prayer book that is used today dates back to the ninth century, when a group of scholars under the leadership of Amram Gaon decided which prayers were most important and planned the present arrangement. Since then there have been many editions of the *Siddur*, but most of them are very close to the original.

Q. *"Why do many synagogues have lions painted or embroidered on the curtains?"*

A.   Each of the twelve tribes of Israel had a symbol, just as the eagle symbolizes the United States. The tribe of Judah used the lion as its symbol. Judah was the bravest and most courageous of Jacob's sons, and out of his tribe came David, Isaiah, Nehemiah, and other great leaders. Because of the importance of this tribe, we frequently see this emblem of the lion as the religious symbol of the entire Jewish people.

Q. *"What is the meaning of the Shield of David?"*

A. Though we are not sure of the origin of the *Magen David*, in recent times it has become a definite religious symbol, found in almost every house of worship. Jewish soldiers buried on the battlefield or in military cemeteries are identified by the Shield of David. In Nazi Europe, Jews were forced to wear yellow arm bands with the *Magen David*. The six-pointed star also symbolizes hope; it is part of the design of the Israeli flag.

Q. *"Why do men wear the prayer shawl at services?"*

A. The *Torah* commands men to make fringes on the four corners of their garments. In Oriental countries the outer garment was a loose robe slipped over the head. The two corners on the front and two on the back had fringes attached to them. Originally, the most important part of each fringe was a thread of blue wool which was intertwined with the rest of the fringe. Since this blue thread was made from a special dye which became unobtainable, the rabbis decided that white wool threads would be sufficient.

Observant Jewish males today still carry out the commandment of wearing fringes as an undergarment, whether praying or not. Others wear the *tallit* with fringes as a shawl only during the time of prayer. The *tallit* has been described as "our uniform of religion."

The fringes on the *tallit* remind us of the many other commandments of Judaism. They also serve as a reminder to be careful of what we do or say. Most Jewish males are buried with the *tallit*, showing their devotion to Judaism even unto death.

Q. *"What are the* tefillin?"

A. The *tefillin*, like the *tallit*, are mentioned in the Bible in connection with the Exodus from Egypt. They remind us daily of our deliverance from slavery. These "phylacteries," as they are called in English, consist of two black boxes attached to leather straps. One box is placed on the arm and the other on the forehead.

Inside the box that fits on the forehead are four scrolls

containing four paragraphs from Exodus and Deuteronomy. There are also four grooves on this box to indicate the division of the scrolls. In the box that fits on the arm these same paragraphs are inscribed on one scroll.

The *tefillin* are placed on the head to encourage us to think wisely, and "between thine eyes" to symbolize the importance of seeking the good. The box on the arm urges us to act righteously.

A modern sage has indicated that the four different scrolls found in the box that goes on the head remind us that Jews are not all required to think alike; when it comes to action, however, symbolized by the arm box, then unity is of greatest importance—hence, one scroll.

Q.   "What does the Eternal Light mean? What happens if it goes out?"

A.   When the Israelites traveled in the wilderness, they were commanded to kindle the Eternal Light. Today it also symbolizes the undying faith of the Jewish people in their God. The light usually hangs over the ark to indicate that the eternal Jewish soul is dependent on the teachings of the *Torah.*

If the Eternal Light happens to go out, it is simply re-kindled as soon as possible.

Q.   "Why are children not counted in a minyan?*"*

A.   Certain prayers can be recited in the synagogue without ten adults present, but such prayers as the *Kaddish* or the reading of the *Torah* require a *minyan*. Only Jewish adults who can fully appreciate the meaning of prayer can be counted as part of a *minyan*.

The rabbis in the Talmud express the opinion that a minimum of ten form a congregation. They derive this opinion from that portion of the Bible dealing with Abraham's pleading to God to save the righteous of Sodom. God finally conceded to save the sinful city if at least ten righteous men could be found there. The rabbis in the Talmud therefore concluded that ten men were a minimum to form a praying congregation. In recent years a growing number of congregations include women in their *minyan*.

The belief continues that unless ten adults gather in a synagogue to recite their prayers in unison, God is not given the respect that is due to Him.

Q.   "Why do most Jews wear hats when they pray?"

A.   As with many other customs, we do not know exactly how this one started. There is no law in the Bible that commands us to cover our heads. In fact, it seems that to do so was a sign of mourning in ancient times. It is even questionable whether the hat was worn in prayer or study by most of the rabbis of the Talmud even though it was considered a symbol of piety to do so.

Eventually this custom which was observed by some became a hard and fast rule among traditional Jews as a symbol of respect for God, whose presence was always before them. Traditional Jews consider it improper to worship or to study the Scripture or Talmud with an uncovered head.

Christians, whose religion developed mainly in the West,

have expressed reverence for God by removing their hats. Reform Jews, likewise, usually remove their hats in the temple.

Q.   *"Why are there no statues or paintings in the synagogue?"*

A.   Originally, it was prohibited to make an image of anything because of the second commandment: "Thou shalt not make unto thee a graven image." The commandment is no longer interpreted in that way, however. We do not find pictures or statues in the synagogue because they tend to distract the worshiper from the prayers, which are directed only to God. We do find figures of lions or flowers on the ark cover or designs in the stained-glass windows.

The Jewish Home and Its Ceremonies

Q. *"What is* Kiddush?"

A.   On the eve of the Sabbath and festivals, the head of the household raises a cup of wine and recites over it the *Kiddush* or "hallowing of the day." The blessing consists first of a prayer of thanks to God for the gift of wine, followed by thanks for the gift of the Sabbath or festival. The head of the household drinks some of the wine and distributes the rest among the members of the family. *Kiddush* is also recited by the cantor in the synagogue on the eve of Sabbath and festivals.

Q. *"Why is wine used for* Kiddush?"

A.   Centuries ago every festive meal began with a cup of wine. Since the Friday evening meal at the beginning of the Sabbath was started with wine, it was proper to recite the prayer announcing the holy Sabbath immediately before drinking that cup of wine. Even after the custom of starting a regular meal with wine was discontinued, the cup of wine before the Sabbath was retained.

Later the symbol of wine became known as a cup of joy, appropriate for welcoming the joyful Sabbath.

Q.   "Why do we light candles for the Sabbath?"

A.   The observance of the Jewish Sabbath and festivals begins before sunset of the day preceding the holy day. Because the Bible prohibited fire to be kindled on the Sabbath, it was an ancient custom for the housewife to kindle the lights before the Sabbath. In time the act of preparing the light to illuminate the house became a religious ceremony.

Today, even though most homes have electric lights, we are still required to follow the ancient custom of kindling the Sabbath lights a short time before sunset. The mother covers her eyes and recites the blessing, "Praised are You, O Lord our God, King of the Universe, who has sanctified us with Your commandments and commanded us to kindle the Sabbath lights." In the absence of the mother, the candles are kindled by someone else in the family.

❖ ❖ ❖

Q.   "Why do some homes use two candles and some three or more?"

A.   It is customary to light at least two candles. At the beginning of the Common Era, the average home had three rooms: a bedroom, living room, and kitchen. During the week two candles were kindled, one for the kitchen and one for the living room. The act of lighting these two candles, which were naturally kindled before the Sabbath, later became a religious act to welcome the Sabbath. Some say that two lights recall the two versions of the Sabbath commandments–"Remember the Sabbath day" and "Observe the Sabbath day."

Some families add a candle for each new member of the family.

Q. *"Why do women cover their eyes when lighting the candles?"*

A.　Ordinarily blessings are recited prior to enjoying a particular pleasure. For instance, we pronounce the blessing over wine before we drink the wine. However, since the blessing over candles marks the beginning of the Sabbath, and since candles cannot be lit once the Sabbath has begun, women light the candles first, then they cover their eyes and recite the blessing, and after this devotional act they enjoy the pleasure of gazing at the candlelight.

Q. *"What is* hallah?"

A.　In the Bible *hallah* was the share of dough that every person had to contribute to the priest when preparing bread for the household. The bread, usually a twisted loaf, that we eat on the Sabbath, is called by the same name, and in some traditional homes in which *hallah* is still baked, the mother burns a small portion as a reminder of the Biblical law.

It is customary to place two *hallot* (plural of *hallah*) on the Sabbath table to commemorate the double portion of manna that the Israelites of the desert gathered on Fridays so that they would have enough food for the Sabbath.

Q. *"Does the* mezuzah *bring good luck?"*

A. Jewish law clearly states that the *mezuzah* is not to be sold or used as an amulet or charm. The command to place the *mezuzah* on the doorpost goes back to the Bible: "And you shall write them upon the doorpost of your house and upon your gates."

Inside the *mezuzah* is a small piece of parchment which includes the *Shema* ("Hear O Israel") and fifteen verses from the book of Deuteronomy. The passage requires us to love God and to serve Him, and reminds us that our children should be instilled with the need to follow the law of God.

The *mezuzah* serves to remind us of God's loving care and also to identify the household as being Jewish.

Q. *"What are* kosher *and* treyfah?"*

A. Any food that is permitted by Jewish law is *kosher*. *Treyfah* refers to food that is unfit or forbidden. Basically the laws of *kashrut* can be summarized as follows:

> All animals that have the split hoof and chew their cud are *kosher*. This excludes such animals as the pig or horse.

Fish that have fins and scales are acceptable. This excludes the shellfish family.

> Animals must be slaughtered by a trained slaughterer *(shohet)* in a way that ensures a speedy death with the least amount of pain. The animal must be free from disease.

> Dairy and meat foods may not be eaten together.

Q. "Why were the dietary laws given to the Jews?"

A.   Undoubtedly health factors were considered to be important. That is why the animals had to meet such rigid health requirements. But the underlying reason for these dietary laws was to promote a more ethical life. The Bible clearly says regarding these laws, "You shall be holy, for I (the Lord) am holy." The dietary laws were intended to make us aware of all God's creation so that even when partaking of permitted animals we should not forget that they are God's creatures. Thus only the most humanitarian means could be used in slaughtering the animals.

According to Maimonides, outstanding Jewish scholar of the twelfth century, people were required to practice self-control in their eating habits so that they could say "no" when other temptations came before them.

Q. "What does mitzvah *mean?"*

A.   The word *mitzvah* (coming from the verb, "to command") is often used to signify a good deed, but it actually has a much greater meaning in Judaism. It is both a commandment and an opportunity given to every Jew to fulfill a law of Judaism so that the individual can better himself or herself and also strengthen the Jewish group.

There are in Jewish life 613 of such *mitzvot* or opportunities, divided into 248 positive and 365 negative commands. Of course, no individual can possibly fulfill all these commands, but we stress the need to fulfill as many as we can. Examples of *mitzvot* are: giving charity, studying *Torah*, and observing the Sabbaths and festivals.

Q. "Does God really reward us for performing mitzvot?"

A. Since most of the *mitzvot* teach us important ethical lessons, our reward is that their observance makes us finer and happier people. Also the observance of one *mitzvah* leads to the observance of others, and we are thus able to improve ourselves.

We should not expect to get material rewards for observance of a *mitzvah*. If we do, then our expecting the reward will become more important to us than the *mitzvah* itself.

Q. "Can one be a good Jew without observing the mitzvot?"

A. There are people who are good and yet do not observe the *mitzvot* of Judaism. They are kind to others, they are fair in their business practices, and they give liberally to charity–and yet they do not see the need to practice formal religion. There is no question about their being good or about their being Jews. However, most people need constant reminders to do good so that if they are tempted to do wrong the routine of practicing the *mitzvot* will help them get on the right path again.

Furthermore, it is questionable whether one can be a good Jew if one is not interested in the survival of his or her people. Without our religious ceremonies in the home and synagogue there would be little to keep us together. A good Jew accepts the responsibilities of furthering Jewish survival by respecting the laws and traditions of Judaism and by seeking the opportunity to observe them.

❖ *Chapter IV*

JEWISH HOLIDAYS AND FESTIVALS
"HOW DO WE CELEBRATE?"

Chapter IV

JEWISH HOLIDAYS AND FESTIVALS

The spirit of Judaism can best be appreciated through an understanding of its year-round holidays. The highlights of Jewish history, the profound concepts of the religion, the joys and sorrows of its people, the techniques of group survival–all find themselves eloquently illustrated in the various holidays.

We can appreciate what Samson Raphael Hirsch, a nine-teenth-century German rabbi, meant when he said, "The catechism of the Jew is his calendar." The essence of Jewish life cannot be transmitted verbally nor can it be sufficiently explained in writing. It must be experienced by living with its rich content transmitted through holiday observance. The calendar, which has not been altered since the fourth century when it was written down, is in itself the product of great genius. Unlike the civil calendar, which is based on the revolution of the earth around the sun, the Jewish calendar is based on a lunar year, the months corresponding with the time it takes the moon to make one revolution around the earth. Since it takes about 365 1/4 days for the earth to travel around the sun, the twelve civil months consist of either thirty or thirty-one days, totaling one entire revolution of the earth. Since it takes the moon about twenty-nine and a half days to revolve around the earth, each Hebrew month consists of either twenty-nine or thirty days, totaling 354 days.

Obviously something had to be done to compensate for the extra days of the solar year; otherwise the holidays would be observed out of their proper season. Therefore, seven times in nineteen years an entire additional month, second *Adar*, is added to the Jewish calendar.

Shabbat

The Sabbath, unlike the holidays that arrive on a fixed day of the month, is not related to the moon. It arrives every seventh day to commemorate God's rest after having created the world.

The importance of the Sabbath is not in the least diminished by its frequency. In fact, its regularity increases its holiness. It takes precedence over all the other holidays except *Yom Kippur*, the Day of Atonement.

The Sabbath alone is mentioned in the Ten Commandments as a day to be observed by all—even the servant, the stranger, and cattle. It has been said that it represents the greatest piece of social legislation in the history of mankind. Our ancients realized that no one could remain productive without rest. Without a Sabbath to culminate their labors, people would lose their self-respect, their dignity, even their desire to work.

The Romans did not realize how advanced the Sabbath institution was. They ridiculed the Jews for wasting away a seventh of their lives in idleness. The Sabbath also interfered with the institution of slavery. The master was not in complete control of his slave; for one day at least the slave was subject to God's will and not to the will of his master.

However, the intrinsic value of the Sabbath goes much

deeper than mere abstention from work. Man (and woman) is bidden to "remember the Sabbath day to keep it holy." He is to give it over to spiritual pursuits, to make the most out of this period of physical rest by elevating himself spiritually and intellectually. He is to set it aside as a day to be observed on a different dimension from that of the usual workaday week—for prayer, joy, and rest.

The many prohibitions connected with the Sabbath are intended to protect the spirituality of the day rather than to create a mood of solemnity for the observant Jew. Our rabbis ordained that funerals were not permitted on the Sabbath; mourning was interrupted so that the Sabbath joy would not be diminished even in an hour of anguish.

Comfort and pleasure are part of Sabbath observance. The Jew is enjoined to sanctify the Sabbath by eating choice meals and wearing his or her best garments. It is a day when both body and soul partake in the rejoicing.

The Sabbath is marked by special songs and elaborate worship in the synagogue on Friday evening and Saturday morning. On Friday evening, whether at a sundown or late service, the *kiddush* over wine is chanted in the synagogue. A portion of the week, one designated for each Sabbath, is read from the *Torah* on *Shabbat*.

At home the Sabbath is usually inaugurated by the mother, who kindles the candles immediately before sunset. In the traditional home the father recites the *Kiddush*, blesses the children, and reads a Biblical passage in honor of the valorous woman. The Sabbath-twist bread *(hallah)*, the special foods, the white tablecloth, and the singing of *zemirot* (songs) all help to enhance the spirituality of the day.

At the conclusion of the Sabbath a ceremony of separation, called *havdalah*, is observed. The Sabbath is bidden farewell with the taste of wine, the fragrance of spices, and the light of a braided candle.

Rosh Hashanah

The Jewish New Year, which ushers in the penitential season, traditionally marks the birthday of the world. Though observed only by Jews, its theme is a universal one. On the two days of *Rosh Hashanah* God's kingship over all people is reaffirmed. We also pray for the time when "everyone will come to serve You and bless Your glorious Name."

The most important symbol of the holy day is the ram's horn or *shofar*, which was used in antiquity for the purpose of calling the people to battle or to announce the fiftieth year jubilee. It was also used at the coronation of the kings of Israel. According to tradition, the *shofar* is linked to the story of the ram who was sacrificed by the patriarch Abraham in his son's stead. It is blown on *Rosh Hashanah* to exhort the people to a life of sacrificial devotion to God and to humankind. Its call is also intended to arouse the people to examine their deeds and to repent for the misdeeds of the past year. During these days of penitence we are required to scrutinize our actions and to make resolutions of self-improvement.

The nature of the holiday is such that the Jew is filled with confidence in his or her ability to change misfortune into blessing, for "prayer, repentance and charity can avert the severe decree."

Yom Kippur

The week following *Rosh Hashanah* is likewise spent in soul-searching and repentance, culminating in the Day of Atonement, *Yom Kippur*, which marks the end of the penitential period. The most significant aspect of the day is the twenty-four hour fast, in which every adult Jew is required to participate. Fasting sincerely observed helps to provide an exalted mood, enabling us to spend a complete day in the atmosphere of the synagogue. It helps us to solidify the people of Israel through a united act. It serves to strengthen us in our struggle to overcome temptation. It teaches us the necessity for self-denial, which is essential to self-improvement.

Moreover, the Day of Atonement reminds us that life is not wholly physical, nor is worldly enjoyment its real aim; that there are higher things by which we live. "Man does not live by bread alone, but by all that cometh out of the mouth of the Lord does man live."

The fast commences with the chanting of *Kol Nidre* by the cantor. This is a prayer in which the congregants ask God to release them from their unfulfilled vows. Though many attempts have been made to delete the prayer from the liturgy because some of the content is not applicable today, the prayer still remains an integral part of the service, largely because of the melody, which sets the solemn mood for the entire day.

The transgressions for which the Day of Atonement helps us to atone are not merely those of ritual character; in fact, greater attention is given to the moral laws which are applicable to all people. Judaism describes different degrees of sin that people are likely to commit, ranging from poor judgment *(het)* to open rebellion against God *(pesha)*. God is prepared to forgive them all, provided that repentance is sincere and that those sins between individuals have been previously settled through mutual forgiveness.

At every service on the Day of Atonement the congregation repeats the Confessional, which contains a list of sins to which the average person is subject: lying, exploiting one's neighbor, stubbornness, etc.–for all these we ask God to pardon and forgive us. The Confessional is recited in the first person plural, indicating one of the basic concepts of Judaism: each of us is responsible for all the sins of our society, either by our own acts of commission or by our passively accepting conditions that lead to crime and lawlessness.

Yom Kippur is replete with historic memories. The *Yizkor* memorial service is recited, calling to mind the passing of dear ones; the Temple service as it was observed two thousand years ago is reenacted by the congregation. The cantor and, in traditional synagogues, the elders even fall to the floor four times in the same way as the community gathered in the ancient Temple used to prostrate itself whenever the Divine Name was pronounced at the service. The most solemn note of the *Yom Kippur* service is struck when the congregation recalls the martyrdom of ten great rabbis who died at the hands of the Romans in the year 135 C.E.

As the sun sets, the fast draws to a close with the *Ne'ilah* service, evoking an image of the gates of repentance that are being closed but reminding us that we still have the opportunity to reconcile ourselves with God through sincere atonement.

Sukkot

Five days after *Yom Kippur*, the Jew is commanded to observe the Feast of Tabernacles. *Sukkot* is one of the three Pilgrimage Festivals, the origin of which dates back to very ancient times. Like *Pesah* and *Shavuot*, it was celebrated as an agricultural festival long before it was associated with any specific events in Jewish history. *Sukkot* was originally a harvest festival at which time the farmer would celebrate the reaping of the seasonal fruit and the gathering of the vintage. The celebration also signified the closing of the agricultural year. It was customary for the farmer to dwell in a booth for protection against wild beasts.

Later the holiday took on a historical meaning. The booths

served to recall the frail shelters that the Hebrews inhabited during their sojourn in the wilderness. Thus it became customary to build temporary quarters every year to recall the Exodus.

A third concept was later incorporated into the meaning of the holiday. The Jew was commanded to express thanksgiving for the bounty of nature. The hut was to be decorated with seasonal fruit to recall gratitude to God for the gifts of nature.

The *Sukkah* serves also to remind us of the frailty of man and his dependence on God for material blessings. The roof is covered with leaves and branches, and the walls are improvised, emphasizing man's mortal nature, his need for God's beneficence. The emphasis was most timely, especially since the farmer, impressed with his abundant crop, might consider himself and not God responsible for his bounteous harvest. He goes forth, then, from his solid home to a frail hut which is vulnerable to floods and winds, thus submitting himself to divine protection and displaying utter trust in God.

Simhat Torah

The ninth day of the autumnal celebration is called *Simhat Torah*, marking the completion of the Five Books of Moses, a portion of which is read in the synagogue each Sabbath of the year. Upon completion of the *Torah* cycle, the Jew expresses unrestrained joy and happiness in the synagogue. The *Torahs* are carried around the synagogue accompanied by spontaneous dancing and singing. In most congregations the worshipers take turns carrying the *Torah*, the children marching with flags and miniature *Torahs*. God is served not only in solemn prayer but also with gaiety. Body and soul combine in praising the Lord.

On *Simhat Torah* day in the traditional synagogue a prominent member is designated as "bridegroom of the *Torah*," and he is called up as the last verses of the Pentateuch are read. Immediately afterwards, so that no hiatus exists between the completion and the beginning, an *aliyah* is given to the "bridegroom of Genesis." And the yearly cycle recommences.

Hanukkah

The Feast of Lights is traditionally a minor holiday. Because of its late origin, it is not mentioned in the Pentateuch. All manner of work is permitted on the eight days of the holiday. And yet, *Hanukkah* has become a holiday of major significance to the Jewish people because it marks the first battle for religious freedom. Time and again the Jewish people have drawn inspiration from the heroic Maccabees who fought valiantly to preserve the Jewish way of life in the face of overwhelming odds.

The Syrio-Greek civilization or Hellenism, with its emphasis on polytheism, its glorification of physical strength, and its insistence on class distinction, attracted the privileged classes of all peoples with whom it came into contact. The Jewish aristocracy was no exception.

It took a brave band of men, realizing that the survival of Judaism was being threatened, to defend their faith against the powerful Syrian armies in the year 168 B.C.E. These patriots were well acquainted with the terrain that they were to defend. But even more important, they were aware that they had a way of life to defend. By the year 165 they had driven the enemy out of Palestine; the demoralized Syrian army did not threaten the homeland again. Judah marched in Jerusalem. His first concern was to rededicate the defiled Temple. Tradition has it that a single cruse of oil was found with the stamp of the High Priest, and the oil miraculously lasted for eight days instead of the anticipated one day. In commemoration of this miracle, eight days of *Hanukkah* were observed by the descendants of the Maccabees.

Our sages were concerned mainly with the spiritual history of the Maccabees; the Talmud discusses the kindling of the lights rather than the battles, for the rabbis considered God's deliverance "of the strong into the hands of the weak, the arrogant into the hands of those devoted to Thy Law" to be of ultimate importance. That is why on the Sabbath of *Hanukkah* we read the prophecy of Zechariah, which concludes with the words: "Not by might, not by strength, but by My Spirit, says the Lord of Hosts."

In recent years the national aspect of the holiday has assumed renewed importance. The battle for Israel's independence in 1949 against the overwhelming Arab armies seemed to indicate that Jewish history was repeating itself. The Jews mustered courage and hope from the Maccabean struggle. Victory would ultimately come to the modern Maccabees and they too would reclaim the land that was rightfully theirs.

On the Feast of Lights, we light candles for eight nights and distribute gifts to children and friends. On the first night of the holiday one candle is lit, on the second night two are lit, and so on, until the last evening, when all eight illuminate the household. Appropriate songs are sung and special prayers are recited for the eight days.

In recent years *Hanukkah* has taken on added meaning for American Jews. New songs, games and pageants, home decorations, and school programs have been developed, much of it superficially stimulated by the challenge of Christmas, which occurs around the same time. Unfortunately, *Hanukkah* has come to be thought of by some Christians and Jews alike as the "Jewish Christmas." Even those who have attempted to explain the nature of the holiday have resorted to apologetics. However, for those who are deeply rooted in the tradition, *Hanukkah* is a holiday of unique significance; its message of right over might is eternally relevant. The heroic struggle of a few dedicated souls will continue to give courage and strength to brave men and women in every age who are concerned with preserving their freedom.

Purim

The Feast of Lots, which usually occurs late in February or March, is also considered to be a minor holiday in the Jewish calendar. Though coupled with *Hanukkah*, it does not commemorate a victory won by the Jewish people against an enemy but rather recalls an escape from destruction through the intervention of God, the bravery of Queen Esther, and the wisdom of Mordecai.

The Book of Esther, commonly known as the *Megillah*, relates in graphic fashion the entire story of Jewish deliverance from Haman, who sought to annihilate the Jews of Persia. The capricious King Ahasuerus, who has been identified by some scholars as Xerxes, acceded to Haman's request and allowed him to cast lots *(pur)* in order to determine the exact day of the mass purge. Mordecai's loyalty to the crown in revealing a plot against the king, as well as Esther's decision to speak in behalf of her people, caused Ahasuerus to reverse his decision; on the day that Mordecai was to have been hanged, Haman and his sons were executed instead.

Each year the *Megillah* is read in an atmosphere of uninhibited gaiety. With each mention of Haman's name, children are permitted to interrupt the reading with noisemakers or *groggers*.

Throughout our long history Haman has represented the prototype of evil. Torquemada and Hitler were called Hamans in modern garb. The inveterate optimism of the Jews in the midst of adversity was to some extent due to the faith that they derived from the *Purim* story. It convinced them that evil had only temporary success and would ultimately succumb to righteousness.

In America, and especially in Israel, carnivals and masquerades centering around the *Purim* theme lend added glamor to the holiday and help to create a mood that is basically Jewish–showing that God may be worshiped not only in the spirit of solemnity, and that sober lessons may be derived even upon occasions when extreme joy is experienced.

Pesah

The Festival of Freedom is by far the most popular Jewish holiday and is probably observed more scrupulously than the Holy Days. One of the reasons for Passover's universal interest is its home character. Members of the family travel great distances to be together at the *Seder* table with their kin. The desire to participate in a *Seder*, no matter where a person may be, indicates that the childhood impressions of the holiday have a fast hold upon the Jewish heart.

Like *Sukkot* and *Shavuot*, *Pesah* was originally a nature festival that later took on historical significance. At one time it commemorated the barley harvest and the lambing season in ancient Palestine; it also marked the rejuvenation of life in general. Eventually, an even greater meaning was attached to the celebration, one characteristic of the Jewish passion for ethics. Passover came to symbolize the Exodus from Egyptian bondage, which meant more than any other single historical event in the life of the ancient Hebrews. It was an exhortation to cherish freedom and liberty as one of the basic requirements of life.

Passover affirms that liberty is the right of every human being as a child of God. To accept subservience to an earthly being is to deny the rule of God. Passover marks the first time that a people challenged the institution of slavery and dared to defy their mortal master to serve a greater Master.

The Israelites, unlike other people, never cared to conceal their humble origin. In fact, they persisted in remembering their slave status so that the difference between serfdom and freedom would remain eternally clear in their minds.

The *Seder*, which is held in traditional households on the first two nights of Passover, highlights the festival. The entire family is seated around the table with the father as teacher and the family as students; it is a class in audio-visual education, each object on the table representing a symbol of the freedom lesson.

The *matzah* is the bread of affliction that our forebears ate in haste while in flight from Egypt. The shankbone represent the paschal sacrifice offered by each family on the eve of Passover. The egg represents an additional sacrifice, but it has also been interpreted to signify the Jewish people—just as the egg hardens when heated, so has the Jewish will to survive become more resolute with each added persecution. The *maror* or bitters remind us of the anguish that the Jews experienced in servitude; the *haroset*, or mixture of apples, nuts, and wine, serves to recall the mortar that the Hebrews were forced to make under the Pharaoh. The greens serve as the symbol of spring. Four cups of wine are drunk at various intervals to recall the four times that God promised freedom to the Israelites. Since the establishment of the State of Israel, a fifth cup has been added in many homes, with an appropriate prayer.

Much of the *Seder* is geared to the interest of the children. The youngest anxiously awaits his or her turn to ask the four questions; they read with the family a description of four different kinds of children and their respective interest in Judaism; they attempt to "steal" the *afikomen* (dessert *matzah*), which is hidden at the beginning of the ceremony. The songs are postponed to the end of the service so that the children's interest will be maintained to the very end.

The *Haggadah*, out of which the family reads the account of Israel's flight to freedom, is a short history of the Jewish people rather than just a description of the holiday. Its passages help to entertain and instruct the more supple minds, to enlighten and to challenge the astute. The principal theme of the entire *Haggadah* is found in the following passage: "In every generation each man must regard himself as though he left Egypt." The Jew is bidden to remind him or herself continually that the task of seeking freedom for the oppressed is never ended. One should never take freedom for granted, and "the more one repeats the story of the Exodus the more praiseworthy he becomes."

Shavuot

The Feast of Weeks, seven weeks after Passover, is celebrated for two days. In Biblical days the Hebrews would count seven weeks from Passover to *Shavuot* by bringing an *omer* or measure of barley to the Temple for forty-nine days, starting with the second evening on Passover, to give thanks to God for their produce during the barley season. In the absence of a written calendar, this was their way of determining the exact date of the Feast of Weeks. Even after the calendar was fixed and the sixth day of *Sivan* was made the date of the holiday, the name Feast of Weeks was retained. In traditional synagogues it is still customary to count the forty-nine days from the second evening of Passover to *Shavuot*.

In time, after the second Temple was destroyed, the Jews

had to rely on their *Torah* to unite them rather than on their land, so they recalled the Ten Commandments that were given to Israel at Mount Sinai. The religious meaning of the holiday thus became more important than the agricultural meaning. *Pesah*, the "freedom *from*" festival, was a prelude to Shavuot–"freedom *for*" receiving God's eternal law. The giving of the *Torah* marked the end of Israel's childhood and its entry into national maturity. At the moment that it accepted the laws of justice, truth, and lovingkindness, Israel secured for itself a permanent existence.

On *Shavuot*, Jews rededicate themselves to the *Torah* by reading the passage containing the Ten Commandments. It is also customary to read the Book of Ruth on the festival of *Shavuot*, since it describes the grain harvest and the treatment of the poor during the harvest season. Ruth also embraces the Jewish faith by accepting the *Torah*.

Other Important Days in the Jewish Year

Tisha Ba' Av, the ninth day of the month of *Av*, commemorates the destruction of the First and Second Temples. In memory of these catastrophes, it is customary among traditional Jews to fast for the entire day. The Book of Lamentations is recited in the evening, and in the morning dirges which record ancient and medieval suffering of the Jewish people.

The minor fasts include *Asarah B'Tevet, Shivah Asar B'Tammuz*, and the *Fast of Gedaliah*–also connected with the loss of the Jewish homeland. *Taanit Esther*, on the day preceding *Purim*, is commemorated in honor of Queen Esther, who fasted for three days before going to Ahasuerus to plead for her people.

Tu Bishevat, the New Year of the Trees, marks the beginning of spring in the Holy Land.

Lag Ba'Omer, which is observed thirty-three days after Passover, commemorates the end of an epidemic that befell the disciples of Rabbi Akiba under the Roman siege. On *Lag Ba'Omer* the Jews recall the bravery of Bar Kochba and his followers who, sixty years after the destruction of the Second Temple, made a courageous effort to regain Palestine from the hands of the Romans.

The following table lists the Jewish holidays, their Hebrew dates, and the months in which they occur on the civil calendar.

Hebrew month and day	*Holiday*	*Month in civil calendar*
Tishri		
1-2	*Rosh Hashanah*	September or October
3	*Fast of Gedaliah*	September or October
10	*Yom Kippur*	September or October
15-16	*Sukkot* (first days)	October
22-23	*Shemini Azeret* ⎱	October
	Simhat Torah ⎰	
Heshvan		
Kislev ⎱		
25		
Tevet ⎰	*Hanukkah*	December
2		
10	*Asarah B'Tevet* (fast)	December or January
Shevat		
15	*Tu Bishevat*	January or February
Adar (Adar II)		
14	*Purim*	February or March
Nisan		
15-22	*Pesah*	March or April
Iyyar		
18	*Lag Ba'Omer*	May
Sivan		
6-7	*Shavuot*	May or June
Tammuz		
17	*Shivah Asar B'Tammuz* (fast)	July
Av		
9	*Tisha Ba'av* (fast)	July or August
Elul		

"How Do We Celebrate?"

One of the essential problems of education in general and of Jewish education in particular is that of applying in the home those attitudes and principles that are taught in the classroom. Just as the child learning about democracy in school must be able to experience its meaning in concrete terms, similarly the Jewish child should be given the opportunity to apply in the home those Jewish attitudes and principles learned in religious school. The teacher in religious school can teach the child to the point of knowing the meaning of the holidays and how to celebrate them, but it is the responsibility of the home to provide the celebration itself.

Home discussions about the Festivals weeks before their actual celebration help the child to build up increased anticipation in addition to a sense of security in knowing that the entire family unit shares the child's enthusiasm.

Q. "How did the Jewish calendar begin?"

A. Our forefathers, who were shepherds in very ancient times, were very aware of the moon. They saw it grow larger each day until it became full and lit up the entire area. Then they saw that it became smaller until it almost disappeared from the sky. They soon learned that it took twenty-nine and one-half days from one moon to another, and they called the period *one moon,* which is the same as one month. They began to count their holidays from the first day of the new moon.

They did not know that the earth revolves around the sun, the principle upon which the regular calendar is based, and even after the new calendar was adopted, the Jews retained their old calendar for religious observances.

Q.   *"Why do Jewish holidays fall on different days each year?"*

A.   The Jewish holidays fall on the same day each year in the Hebrew calendar. The civil calendar is determined by the sun (solar), and the earth revolves around the sun about every 365 days instead of the 354 (29 1/2 x 12) days of the moon year. Therefore the Jewish holidays come on different dates in the solar calendar every year.

Q.   *"Doesn't the Hebrew calendar lose quite a few days each solar year according to this counting?"*

A.   Exactly. That is why the Hebrew calendar has a leap month called *Adar Sheni* ("second *Adar*"), which occurs seven times every nineteen years, to make up for the lost days. Otherwise, holidays like Passover would slip back about eleven days every year. After ten years it would slip back 110 days and would take place in January. It is most important that Passover come out in the spring every year, for the Bible requires it to be celebrated at that time, and furthermore many of the ceremonies connected with Passover deal with the theme of spring.

Q.   *"How do we figure out what Hebrew year we are in now?"*

A.   If you want to know what year it is according to the Jewish calendar, just add 3760 years to the year we are now in according to our everyday calendar. Thus 1991 would correspond to the Hebrew year 5751 (3760 plus 1991).

Q.   "Why do some of our holidays last for two days?"

A.   Actually the Jews who lived in ancient Israel celebrated only one day because they knew the exact day of the
new moon, which was announced by the Supreme Court
(*Sanhedrin*) in Jerusalem. But the people outside of Israel
could not be sure, since it took weeks before the messengers
would reach them to announce the exact day that the holiday
was to be celebrated. They were therefore instructed to
observe festivals for two days instead of one in order to be
sure that the correct day would be included.

Later, when the exact day could be determined by means
of astronomy, the Jews outside of Israel retained their custom
because it gave them an added day of rest from their labors,
just as people welcome a July Fourth weekend today, adding
an extra day to their vacation. So to this very day Jews in
Israel observe one day of *Shavuot* and, with the exception of
Reform Jews, those outside of Israel observe two days.

Sabbath

Q.   "Why does the Sabbath begin at sunset?"

A.   The custom of starting the Sabbath at sunset is based
on the story of creation: "And it was evening and it was
morning, the first day." The day commenced with the
evening. The Sabbath then is ushered in with sunset on
Friday and ends after sundown on Saturday.

Usually the Sabbath lasts for about twenty-five hours,
since it is considered proper to begin the holiday before

sunset with the lighting of the candles. We rush to welcome the Sabbath but are slow to bid it farewell.

Q. *"Is Sabbath another word for Saturday?"*

A. No, though the Jewish Sabbath falls on Saturday, they do not mean the same thing. Saturday comes from the word *Saturn* and Sabbath is derived from the word *Shabbat*, which means rest.

Q. *"What is special about Shabbat rest?"*

A. We not only rest our bodies but also our minds from the things that we do all week long. First of all, we are supposed to take our time on *Shabbat*. We may have to rush through our meals during the week, but on the Sabbath the family spends more time around the table. We also spend more time in prayer, in singing, in reading. We try to bring out the best that is in us on *Shabbat*.

God ordained the Sabbath for us because He knows that we cannot really be happy if we do not change our routine at least once a week. We are told by our rabbis that the Jew has another soul that takes over on the Sabbath. That is to say, we are or should try to be our best selves on *Shabbat*.

Q. *"What is an Oneg Shabbat?"*

A. When the famous Hebrew poet Hayyim Nahman Bialik came to Palestine before Israel became a Jewish state, he would hold a public gathering in his home every Sabbath.

He called this gathering *Oneg Shabbat* or "Sabbath's delight." This practice became popular in other parts of the world and was adopted by many synagogues in our country. Either on Friday evening after the service or on Saturday afternoon people gather together for discussion and social enjoyment in the spirit of *Shabbat*.

Q. "Were the Jews the first people to keep the Sabbath?"

A. The Israelites were the first people to keep the Sabbath as a day of rest and enjoyment in the presence of family and friends. It is possible, however, that the Israelites learned about the way that the Mesopotamians saw the seventh day as bringing bad luck. Their king was not permitted to eat cooked meat, change his clothes, or ride in his chariot on every seventh day of certain months, because he couldn't take chances that something dreadful would happen to him.

The Israelites rejected any superstition connected with the seventh day; by observing a day of rest each week, they were following God's example when He "rested" on the seventh day after creating the world.

Q. "How can the Sabbath be a pleasure when there are so many 'don'ts' that we are expected to obey?"

A. When the rabbis set down the different prohibitions for the Sabbath, their intention was not to create hardships but rather to help us derive the most out of the Sabbath. For instance, it is forbidden to cook or bake on the Sabbath. If a mother prepares her food before the Sabbath, she will have the day free to spend with her family in the synagogue and at home. The prohibition against shopping and sewing also helps to make the Sabbath more enjoyable by freeing it from weekday routines.

Q.   *"If the Sabbath is so important, why don't more people observe it?"*

A.   Many people think that the Sabbath is not important because it comes so often. They take it for granted, just as they overlook other gifts of life that come to them regularly, such as food and clothing.

Others would like to keep the Sabbath, but they must work to make a living since the majority of Americans do not regard Saturday as their day of rest. There are a good number of devoted Jews who still manage to observe the Sabbath. Since, in recent years, many businesses and offices are closed on Saturday, these people manage to obtain jobs that do not require their working on the Sabbath.

Others observe as much as they can. The story is told about a soldier who was going overseas during the war. He went to his rabbi to ask him how he could keep the Sabbath in the heat of battle. His rabbi told him to differentiate the day from others, if only by shooting one bullet less on the Sabbath. What he meant was that the soldier should not forget *Shabbat* even when in combat, and upon return, it would be easier to follow his old way of life.

Q.   *"Why don't we observe Sunday as our Sabbath?"*

A.   It may be true that Sunday would be a more convenient day on which to observe the Sabbath since most people do not work on that day, but experience has taught the Jews that any such attempt is unsuccessful. The seventh day has special memories for the Jew, who for centuries has struggled to keep it as a sacred day. A people cannot forget its history just for the sake of convenience.

It is in part the struggle to maintain the seventh day as our own Sabbath that has made it so dear to us; in turn the observance of the seventh day as the Sabbath has kept the Jews together. One great writer has said: "More than Israel kept the Sabbath the Sabbath kept Israel."

Rosh Hashanah

Q. "What does Rosh Hashanah *mean?"*

A. *Rosh Hashanah* means "head of the year." According to our tradition, the month of *Tishri* marks the birth of the world.

To the Jews New Year's cannot be celebrated with drinking and merrymaking. It is a more serious occasion, when we must recall that God alone was responsible for the world's coming into being and when we must pay our allegiance once again to the King of the Universe. In a way we take part in the King's coronation every *Rosh Hashanah*.

But we must realize that God is more than King of the world; He is also the Judge of the world. At the New Year we come before this Great Judge with the hope that we have improved ourselves over the past year, and we pledge to do even better in the year to come.

Q. "Why is the blowing of the shofar *so important?"*

A. The *shofar* or ram's horn is a very old instrument that goes back to shepherd days. Among other uses, it was a call to arms, to bring the people together in a general emergency, and to announce such important events as the crowning of the king. Tradition has it that we blow the *shofar* on *Rosh Hashanah* to call the people to make sacrifices for the sake of their ideals and beliefs. There are three basic notes that are blown, each call symbolizing a different mood. One is a symbol of happiness, another of sadness, and a third sounds the alarm. Every person is expected to know when to be sad, when to be happy, and when to be on guard.

In general, the *shofar* is the call to our conscience to take over and guide us in our actions.

Yom Kippur

Q. *"Why is* Yom Kippur *called the most important day in the Jewish calendar?"*

A. In ancient times it was only on *Yom Kippur* that the High Priest alone entered the Holy of Holies where the spirit of God was thought to dwell. Even though this sacred ceremony was discontinued with the destruction of the Temple, *Yom Kippur* is to this day the holiest of days. The twenty-four hour fast and all the hours spent in prayer are intended to make us feel closer to God than at any other time during the year. Our thoughts and prayers are directed to the seriousness of life, the proper relations between one person and another, and between a person and God.

And yet, as serious as the holiday is, we know that God forgives us for our sins, and we can start afresh at the end of the holiday. This thought makes us happier.

Q. *"Why do adults fast on* Yom Kippur?"

A. Fasting puts us in a serious mood, a mood that is

proper when praying for forgiveness. By fasting we show God that we are willing to give up at least a day's meals, and to give serious thought to our conduct.

Q. *"What does* Kol Nidre *mean?"*

A. Often we will vow to ourselves to do or not do certain things, and we find that it becomes difficult to keep our promise. Our conscience begins to hurt us because we do not like to break vows made even in private. *Kol Nidre*, then, gives us the chance to cancel these vows since God realizes that we attempted to keep them but could not.

Q. *"The word 'sin' is mentioned in the prayer book time and again. What does it mean to the Jew?"*

A. To sin is to do that which is not good. It is to think about our own wants before God's wants and to neglect the needs of others. No individual, not even the greatest, can live a life that is free from sin, for if that were possible, a human being would be like God. But Judaism teaches that every person is able to live a life that is basically good if he or she chooses to cooperate with God. And when the person does commit a sin, he or she may, through repentance, be able to repair its damage and avoid its repetition.

Q. *"Do we 'confess' in the same way as the Catholics?"*

A. They too ask forgiveness for their sins by confession, but Catholics confess their sins to another human being, the priest of the church. Jews confess directly to God. Furthermore, Jews not only confess for their own sins but ask forgiveness for the sins of all people. That is why in the Confessional we say, "we have sinned" and not "I have sinned."

Q.   *"Why didn't God make us perfect in the first place?"*

A.   If God had made us perfect, then there would be no room for improvement, and we would have no goals to work for. Just as the game of football could not be played without goalposts so life would be dull and useless without goals to achieve. The wish to do better each day brings us closer and closer to God, who is all-good.

Sukkot and Simhat Torah

Q.   *"Is the American Thanksgiving taken from the Sukkot festival?"*

A.   Yes. After the Pilgrims came to America they were grateful to God for their new home. They were thankful for having survived the first hard winter, they had sufficient meat and corn and preserves, and their stores were full for the next winter. They therefore followed the Biblical custom of celebrating a harvest festival and thereby showing their thanks to God for His many gifts.

Q.   *"Does the observance of* Rosh Hashanah, Yom Kippur *and* Sukkot *in such close succession have any special meaning?"*

A.   Actually the three are separate holidays, but taken

together they teach a very important lesson. *Rosh Hashanah* marks the birthday of the world in the Jewish tradition and reminds us of our responsibility to humanity and to God, who is Creator of the universe. *Yom Kippur* deals largely with the individual, who asks God to forgive him for his personal sins against Him. *Sukkot* is a national holiday recalling the history of our people and reminding us of our duties to the Jewish people and to God, who brought us to our freedom and made us a people. When we are aware that we must show concern for humanity and our people as well as with our inner righteousness, then we have learned one of the most important lessons in Judaism.

Q.   *"Why is the roof of the Sukkah not entirely covered?"*

A.   The temporary home for many Jews during the *Sukkot* festival is known as a *Sukkah*. There they eat their meals with family and friends and sing songs to celebrate one of the most joyous holidays of the year.

According to our tradition, when one sits in the *Sukkah* he or she must be able to see the stars overhead. Doing this teaches us that even though we are sitting within our own walls, which symbolize Jewish life, we must be concerned with the universe and with humanity, of which we are a vital part.

Q.   *"Why is the booth so frail?"*

A.   A great lesson is learned from the frailty of the *Sukkah*. You may have heard someone say, "I'm a self-made person; I owe my success to myself." Well, no one is entirely self-made. We all need God more than many of us know, since He is the source of our blessings.

There are other people who are so impressed with their greatness that they think they will live forever. The fragile, temporary *Sukkah* teaches us how frail we really are; even the most powerful will some day pass on.

In other words, Judaism tells us that the human being is not helpless; a person can accomplish great things in life. But if people realize that God is the Source of their strength, then they will not desire to take advantage over others and hurt them because of their own temporary power.

Q. *"Why are the* lulav *and* etrog *used?"*

A. The *lulav* (palm branch) is joined together with the myrtle on one side and willow on the other. With the *etrog* (citron), four types of growing things are represented. By placing these four species together we recall with gratitude all the things that come from the soil.

During the recital of the *Hallel* service, which includes psalms of praise to God, the *lulav* and *etrog* are taken in hand and at certain portions of the prayer they are moved to and fro eastward, southward, westward, northward, upward, and downward, to show that God, who is being thanked for His gifts, is found everywhere.

Q. *"Why is* Simhat Torah *(the 'Rejoicing of the Law') held after* Sukkot *rather than on* Shavuot, *when the* Torah *was given?"*

A. It is true that the *Torah* was given to Israel in the month of *Sivan*, according to tradition, but the people of Israel did not know its contents. It is only after the *Torah* is read and studied that we can truly celebrate. And since the *Torah* cycle is completed on *Simhat Torah*, we hold the appropriate celebration at that time.

Similarly, we seldom recall the birthdays of great Jews but rather the anniversaries of their death. It is at the completion of a great person's life that we are able to tell how great the person really was. So it is with the *Torah*–we really appreciate it only after we have studied it.

Hanukkah

Q.   *"Why couldn't the Jews live happily as a minority among their Syrian neighbors as we in America live?"*

A.   The Syrians did not practice democracy, and minorities can be happy only when they live in a land where they are respected as equals. The Syrians were influenced by the Greeks and their way of life, which was called "Hellenism." This Greek civilization was in some ways helpful to Judaism in that we learned many fine ideas from it, but by and large it contradicted the Jewish way of life. First, the Greeks worshipped many gods–a god of love, of war, of wine, and many others. A number of wealthy Jews found this worship of many gods attractive. Because of this split of allegiance, the Jews of ancient Israel were becoming divided and their strength was being lost. Also the Syrian-Greeks insisted on the continuation of slavery, which the Jews were discouraging since it was against God's will.

For these and other reasons, the Jews knew that they had to shake off the yoke of Hellenism. Therefore they rebelled against their masters.

Q.   "Is Hanukkah then celebrated because of the military victory over the Syrians?"

A.   *Hanukkah* recalls more than a military victory. It is a victory of right over might. Strength is not as important to God as goodness, and He protects the good people from the powerful. That is why during this holiday we read the prophecy of Zechariah, who declared: "Not by might nor by power, but by My Spirit, says the Lord of Hosts." And in the Silent Devotion we add: "You did deliver the strong into the hands of the weak and the haughty into the hands of those devoted to Your Law."

Q.   "Why do we celebrate the minor holiday of Hanukkah for eight days?"

A.   One reason given for the eight days' celebration of *Hanukkah* is the familiar story about the flask of oil that miraculously lasted for eight days instead of one. Some scholars have pointed out that the Maccabees could not celebrate the holiday of *Sukkot* in its proper time because they were in the thick of battle. They therefore celebrated *Hanukkah*, a second *Sukkot*, for eight days after the battle for Jerusalem was won. That is why, they say, the *Hallel* service is recited all eight days of *Hanukkah* just as it is recited for the eight days of *Sukkot*.

Q.   "Why is it customary to play games on Hanukkah?"

A.   Hundreds of years ago it was customary to play chess while the *Hanukkah* lamps were burning because the moves in this game are like military tactics, symbolizing the strategy of Judas Maccabee. Later on, other games were introduced, the stakes usually being candies, nuts, and raisins. The most familiar of these amusements is the *dreidle* game played with a top.

Q.   *"What do the letters on the* dreidle *mean?"*

A.   Each letter stands for a Hebrew word, and together they form the sentence: *Nes gadol hayah sham , "a great miracle was there."*

In Yiddish each of the four letters stands for a different word, upon which the *dreidle* game is based. "N" means *nichts,* or "nothing"; "G" stands for *gantz,* or "everything"; "H" means *halb,* or "half"; "SH" means *shtel,* or "put out."

Tu Bishevat

Q.   *"Is* Tu Bishevat *a new holiday?"*

A.   No. Many years ago trees were planted on that day. For every boy born during the year, a cedar, being one of the strongest trees that grow in Israel, was planted. For every girl, a cypress tree was planted because of its beauty. When a boy and girl were married, branches of their trees would be cut down to build their marriage canopy.

Q.   *"Why do we celebrate* Tu Bishevat *or Israel's Arbor Day?"*

A.   We who live in the United States cannot begin to realize how necessary trees are to a country that suffers from a shortage of them. In Israel, trees are essential to give shade and protection from the hot desert sun. They provide fruit for eating and lumber for building. Certain trees, such as the eucalyptus, which need a great deal of water because of their thick roots, help to dry up the dangerous swamps. For hundreds of years the land of Israel was neglected, and the impoverished people who lived there did not think about planting trees.

American Jews have had millions of trees planted in Israel through such projects as the Jewish National Fund. This is one of the many ways in which we can show our concern for our brothers and sisters in the old-new land.

Q.   *"How do American Jews celebrate the holiday?"*

A.   There are no religious services connected with *Tu Bishevat*. We usually celebrate the day by eating some of the fruit that is grown in Israel, among them St. John's bread, and by sending money for trees to be planted there. Usually religious schools hold assemblies on that day and sing beautiful songs that were written for the occasion.

Purim

Q.   *"Are the Book of Esther and the* Megillah *the same?"*

A.   Yes. There are five *Megillot* or short scrolls in the Bible (not to be confused with the *Torah*-scroll) that are read at different times during the year. Because this scroll of Esther is the most popular of the five, it is often called *The Megillah*. This *Megillah*, which contains the *Purim* story, is read on the eve of *Purim* and on *Purim* day.

Curiously, the name of God is not mentioned in the entire

Megillah. We do not know the exact reason for the omission, although we do know that it was left out purposely. However, the book is still sacred to the Jew.

Q. *"Isn't is disrespectful to make noise in the synagogue as we do on* Purim?"

A. It is disrespectful to make noise at the wrong time. To speak at length with one's neighbor during a regular service is considered improper, but when custom permits us to make noise, then it is not wrong to do so, even in the synagogue.

Q. *"Shouldn't we have forgiven Haman's wickedness by now? Why then do we still drown out his name with noises?"*

A. It may seem strange, but in Israel effigies of Haman are still burned today, and at *Purim* masquerades he is the target of abuse. We are concerned not so much with the Haman of Persia who attempted to kill the Jews, but rather with all the anti-Semites in every age and in every country, whom Haman has come to represent. On *Purim,* we recall all those bigots who wanted to annihilate the Jewish people. The *Purim* story has given us the courage to resist the Hamans and the hope that God would again deliver us. Because of this, our sages have said: "When all the festivals will be observed no more, *Purim* will still remain."

Q. "Is Purim *celebrated in any special way in Israel?"*

A. Yes, especially in Tel Aviv, where the whole city turns out for a carnival. It is called *adloyada,* the Hebrew for "until one cannot tell the difference" (between Haman and Mordecai). A great parade with attractive floats passes through the main streets of the city. Other cities and villages send a special float to represent them. Some display their farm products and others their industrial achievements. The most beautiful girl, who has been chosen as Queen Esther, leads the parade. Following the floats are the men, women, and children dressed in costumes. In the opera house there is a masque ball, in addition to the many private celebrations that are held in the spirit of the occasion.

Pesah

Q. "What does Pesah *really mean?"*

A. *Pesah* means "paschal lamb," sacrificed and partaken of by the Israelites on the eve of their departure from Egypt. The lamb was sacred to the Egyptians, and its blood, sprinkled by the Israelites on their own doorposts, symbolized defiance to the Egyptian gods and all their religious traditions. The paschal lamb was offered regularly at this season during the days of the Temple in memory of their departure.

Q. "Why is all hametz *cleared from the home before Passover?"*

A. Doing this reminds us of the unleavened bread or *matzah* that was baked in haste as our ancestors left the land of the Pharaoh. Observant Jews attach such importance to this event that they refrain from eating not only leavened bread but any food that might have a taste or trace of leaven. We are bidden to put ourselves in the position of the slaves for eight days by tasting their "bread of affliction," as *matzah* is called. By recalling their suffering and their departure, we are expected to remember this most important event in the life of our people.

❖ ❖ ❖

Q.   "Why don't Jews sacrifice animals today?"

A.   Ever since the Second Temple was destroyed by the Romans in 70 C.E., we discontinued the practice of the sacrifice of animals; without the Temple there was no longer a central place to perform these sacrifices. The Jews were told by their leader Rabbi Johanan ben Zakkai that charity and good deeds were just as important in the eyes of God as sacrifices and that the people need not feel that they were neglecting God's law.

Interestingly enough, a small sect of Samaritans who still live together in Israel continue to sacrifice a lamb on Passover just as the Bible required.

Q.   "What is the Haggadah?"

A.   *Haggadah* means "telling" or "narrative." As this name implies, it *tells* of the events leading up to and including the Exodus from Egypt, starting with the dawn of Jewish history. Also included in the *Haggadah* are directions for arranging the Passover plate and the procedure for the *Seder* ceremony. The *Haggadah* was not always used at the *Seder*. In very ancient times the father would relate the story of Passover to the children. The book that we use today developed over a period of many years.

Q. "What does Seder *mean?"*

A. *Seder* means "order." Each step of the *Seder* was carefully planned many centuries ago. The order of the *Seder* ceremony is found at the beginning of the *Haggadah*. The *Seder* ceremony is both a continuation of the ancient ceremony of sacrificing the paschal lamb and a fulfillment of the Biblical command to retell the story of the Exodus to one's children.

Q. "Why do children play so important a part at the Seder?"

A. The Bible says clearly concerning the Passover story: "And you shall tell it to your son." "And it shall come to pass, when your children say unto you." The Talmud states that the *Seder* is planned especially to impress the children. Since the Exodus is one of the most significant events in Jewish history and the meaning of freedom is so important in the Jewish religion, every effort is made at the *Seder* to impress the children so that they will always remember and teach the same story to their own children in later years. The songs that the children have learned are sung at the end of the *Seder* so that they will not fall asleep before the service is over.

The *Seder*, however, is not only for the sake of the children. It is for the entire family. That is why the *Haggadah* states that even though we may be wise and advanced in years, we should continue to retell the story of Passover. In fact, the next paragraph in the *Haggadah* tells of four of the greatest scholars who stayed up all night recalling the Exodus, and they were so interested in the subject that they had to be reminded that it was time to recite the morning prayers.

Q.   "Are the four questions answered anywhere?"

A.   Though they are not answered directly, replies are given throughout the *Haggadah*. A bright child would naturally ask the same kind of questions even if they were not mentioned in the *Haggadah*, but to prompt the younger children, four leading questions have been formed.

Brief answers to the four questions are as follows: (1) We eat only unleavened bread to remind us of the bread that the Israelites baked in haste as they fled from the Egyptians. (2) We eat only bitter herbs to recall the bitterness that our fathers experienced under the rule of the Pharaoh. (3) We dip greens into salt water to remind us of the spring season of the year, and bitters into *haroset* (the mixture of nuts, apples, and wine) to recall the anguish of our people. (4) We recline at the *Seder* table because we are free today.

Q.   "Why is Elijah remembered on Passover?"

A.   There are many legends about Elijah the Prophet and how he assisted the poor and unfortunate in his time. We are reminded on Passover to show the same kindness to those who are hungry and who are not fortunate enough to have their own family *Seder*, by inviting them to be with us.

Elijah, according to a Jewish legend, is to announce the coming of the Messiah. When he reappears, we shall know that the age of peace is at hand. On *Seder* night, Jews express renewed hope for redemption from exile and for the rebuilding of the Jewish homeland. For these reasons Elijah's cup is filled at the *Seder* table and the door is left open to welcome him.

Q.   *"Why is the period after Passover a period of mourning?"*

A.   After the Temple was destroyed in 70 C.E., the Jews revolted against the tyranny of Rome. Leaders of the revolt were Bar Kochba, an able general, and Akiba, a famous scholar.

Though the Jews were successful at first, Rome proved too mighty. Her tremendous army overran the Jewish homeland, putting an end to the last attempt, until modern times, to rebuild the Jewish State.

During the revolt, according to tradition, a terrible epidemic struck the students of Akiba. No less than 24,000 young men lost their lives. Therefore, these weeks were declared a period of mourning when no festivities such as weddings could take place.

Lag Ba'Omer

Q.   *"Why do we engage in sports on Lag Ba'Omer?"*

A.   It has become customary to observe *Lag Ba'Omer* with outings and sport activities because of a legend about the great teacher, Simeon ben Yochai, who lived during the revolt against Rome. Simeon refused to obey the Roman decree against the study of *Torah*, and he continued to teach his pupils in a cave. For thirteen years he lived with his son in a cave, eating merely from the fruit of a carob tree. His students would disguise themselves as hunters carrying bows and arrows so that the Romans would not question their destination. Simeon died on *Lag Ba'Omer*, requesting that the day of his death be celebrated rather than mourned. To this day we observe the holiday by taking field trips and participating in competitive games.

Shavuot

Q.   "Are the Ten Commandments important only for the Jews?"

A.   They are important not only to the Jews but to all the people of the world as the foundation for every civilized community and every society. It is for this reason, say the rabbis, that they were given in the desert, in territory belonging to no one people, but to everyone.

Every country has its particular constitution. The Ten Commandments are, in a way, a world constitution, a code of moral laws for all civilized people. Almost every great book that has been written on morality contains ideas that can be traced back to the original Ten Commandments.

Yet, the Ten Commandments are not intended to tell us all of our obligations. They contain, rather, the least that all people can do if they wish to live a good life.

Q.   "Did the Jewish people choose to accept the Ten Commandments, or were they forced upon them?"

A.   According to tradition, God offered the Ten Commandments to other people first, but they could not accept such commands as "Thou shalt not steal." The Hebrews, however, answered God: "All that the Lord has spoken we will do and we will obey."

Another legend, however, has it that God forced the Hebrews to accept the *Torah*, lifting the mountain above their heads. One teacher explained the contradiction in the following way: often we are forced to undertake certain responsibilities in life, but later we learn to love them so much that we follow them as if we had chosen them in the first place. A mother has a duty to take care of her child, but her love becomes so great that it is as though it were voluntary. So the Hebrews accepted the *Torah* and grew to love it as if they had accepted it voluntarily.

Q.   *"Where are the Ten Commandments found?"*

A.   The Ten Commandments are found in the Bible in Exodus and Deuteronomy. The passage in Exodus is repeated on the first day of *Shavuot*. They may also be found after the daily morning service in many standard prayer books, but they are not recited as part of any traditional service.

At one time they were recited as part of the *Shema* portion of the daily service, but when some people claimed that all they had to do is follow the Ten Commandments and not the rituals of Judaism, the rabbis made the Ten Commandments a supplement to the prayers. The *Shema*, containing the laws of *mezuzah* and *tefillin* in addition to some of the same ideas found in the Ten Commandments, became the central prayer.

Q.   *"Are there any special foods for* Shavuot?*"*

A.   It is customary to eat dairy foods and honey for *Shavuot*. One of the reasons for the custom has been derived from the Biblical passage, "honey and milk shall be under thy tongue," implying that the words of the *Torah* may be as pleasant to our ears and hearts as milk and honey are to the tongue.

Q.   "Is there any special Shavuot *celebration in America?"*

A.   Yes. Reform Jews introduced the ceremony of Confirmation some years ago in which children of fifteen or sixteen years became formally inducted into the family of Israel after having completed a course of study in the Sunday school. This special ceremony replaced the individual *Bar Mitzvah* for boys and also included the girls.

In recent years the individual *Bar Mitzvah* has been restored in a growing number of Reform Congregations, and the *Bat Mitzvah* has been introduced.

In time, many Conservative congregations also adopted the Confirmation for girls. In some Conservative congregations the Confirmation has become the ceremony marking the completion of Hebrew school for both boys and girls in addition to *Bar* and *Bat Mitzvah*. The confirmands stand on the altar and participate in the *Shavuot* service. They declare their loyalty to Judaism and pledge themselves to follow the law of Moses that was given to Israel at this season.

Q.   "Is Shavuot *celebrated differently in Israel than in America?"*

A.   In addition to the synagogue service, there is a special celebration in Israel by the farm communities. The finest produce of the season is loaded on trucks or wagons and brought to a huge amphitheater in the city. The children, dressed in white and carrying flowers and branches, form a procession. After each farming colony or *kibbutz* places its offerings on the platform of the theater, the fruit is sold and the money is given to the Jewish National Fund, which leases land to newcomers. This colorful and meaningful ceremony is called *bikkurim* (first fruits) and calls to mind the ancient *bikkurim* ceremony celebrated in ancient Israel.

After the ceremony, the children usually participate in a pageant dramatizing some *Shavuot* theme.

❖ *Chapter V*

JUDAISM AND ITS MORAL CONCERNS
"CAN I DECIDE WHAT IS RIGHT FOR ME?"

Chapter V

Judaism and Its Moral Concerns

Invariably critics of religion indicate that their main objection to ritual observance is that it is not related to practicing morality. They furthermore cite the "religious people" they know who manage to separate their religious behavior from the way they choose to conduct their business.

The chapter on religious duties and practices discussed the different functions that Jewish rituals serve. It is true that the observance of certain Jewish rituals are not intended primarily to improve our character, unless we regard discipline and obedience to a higher law as character building. Yet, the function of most commandments, especially those between one person and another, are clearly meant to improve our character and sensitize us to make moral decisions.

How do we find the direction that helps us to avoid decisions that hurt ourselves and others? In addition to the Hebrew Bible, the world's greatest repository of ethical insights, the Jewish people has also inherited the vast literature of the Talmud, composed by practical-minded scholars who were primarily students of ethics. These sages devoted themselves to interpreting the Torah and applying its timeless moral truths to their daily lives. These Talmudic sages were free to expand the interpretations of the Torah in order to clarify what the Torah might have understated.

We can learn about some of their moral priorities in the following passage, which is from *Talmud Shabbat* and is also repeated in the daily prayer book.

These are the deeds which yield immediate fruits and continue to yield fruit in the time to come: honoring parents; doing deeds of lovingkindness; attending the house of study punctually, morning and evening; providing hospitality; visiting the sick; helping the needy bride; attending the dead; probing the meaning of prayer; making peace between one person and another, and between man and wife. And the study of the Torah is most basic to them all.

Based on *Talmud Shabbat*, 127A

Although showing lovingkindness appears to be just one among a number of meritorious acts, most of these acts are included under the single theme of practicing *gemilut hasadim* or acts of lovingkindness, one of the highest forms of morality. The Rabbis further explain why acts of lovingkindness are so special in the Jewish scale of values.

Deeds of lovingkindness are superior to charity in three respects. Charity can be accomplished only with money; deeds of lovingkindness can be accomplished through personal involvement as well as money. Charity can be dispersed only to the needy; deeds of lovingkindness can be done for the rich and the needy. Charity applies only to the living; deeds of lovingkindness apply to the living and the dead.

Sukkah, 49B

The primary interest of these sages was not to enunciate abstract principles. Since most of them were gainfully employed, living and working in the community, they offered their practical wisdom when moral decisions were to be made.

Here is a small sampling of suggestions intended to help people make moral decisions. They are taken from the *Mishna Avot*, or Ethics of the Fathers.

He [Hillel] used to say, If I am not for myself, who will be for me? And if I am only for myself, what am I? And if not now, when? (1:14)

Comment: Hillel here emphasizes the value and necessity of self-interest. It is unrealistic to expect others to take care of our needs. If we don't care for ourselves, who will? And yet, we cannot make self-interest our only concern. If we are out only to please ourselves, we become totally self-centered, unable to appreciate the needs of others and our interdependence. Hillel then urges us to accept these two compatible principles and to act upon them without procrastination. Timing is essential in making a wise moral decision.

Rabbi (Judah the Prince) said, Which is the right course a person should choose for himself? That which is honorable to him who does it, and which also brings him honor from mankind. (2:1)

Comment: Rabbi Judah advises that, before making a momentous decision, one should pose two questions to oneself: Will my action bring me personal satisfaction and enhance my sense of self-esteem? Will my decision also be sanctioned by the community. If both needs will be satisfied, then the decision is probably a wise one and should be pursued.

Rabbi Eliezer said: Let the honor of your fellow man be as dear to you as your own. (2:15)
Rabbi José said: Let the property of your fellow man be as dear to you as your own. (2:17)

Comment: Both sages are concerned with the way we are expected to regard other people—their character and their material possessions. Both views should be understood as one unit.

Although it is difficult to give others the same sense of

priority that we give to ourselves, morality demands that we do. Otherwise we will more likely give ourselves the advantage at another's expense because *our* status and *our* possessions become more important. Therefore, even if we can't love our neighbor as intensely as we love ourselves, we should not differentiate between his personal status and ours, his property and ours. We are the guardians and custodians of our neighbor's reputation and the things that belong to him.

"Can I Decide What Is Right for Me?"

Parents are naturally concerned with telling their children about right and wrong at a very early age, long before they enter the classroom. However, the questions of how to teach ethics to young children is not simple. Should the child learn that stealing is wrong only after having taken something without permission, or should the child be told that stealing is wrong before being tempted? Actually, the child should be taught ethical concepts as soon as he or she can grasp their meaning. There is no law that requires the child to go through a stealing or lying stage of development.

The feeling of being denied free will can begin at an early age. Even if the child perceives that a choice between right and wrong is restricted, a perception not necessarily based on reality, then the child may begin to see himself as a victim of circumstances beyond his control, not as one who is capable of making a moral decision independently. When a young boy complains that his friend forced him to shoplift with him, or a girl claims she couldn't refuse to share her test answers with the girl next to her, they are denying that they have the ability to make crucial decisions on their own. Such an attitude could remain with a child through adulthood unless it is challenged at an early age.

Once the child can be convinced that he or she, and no one else, has the freedom to say yes or no when confronted with a moral decision, then the child feels a greater sense of responsibility and accepts the challenge to make the right choice.

Q.   *"Am I always supposed to know when I am about to do the wrong thing?"*

A.   No. Sometimes we have to make the mistake so that we can learn not to repeat it.

There are times, however, when the first mistake can be harmful to us. For example, certain drugs may be hard to resist after their first use. We shouldn't feel ashamed to ask our parents before or after a step that could be harmful.

Q.   *"Why can't people choose what they want to do with their own bodies?"*

A.   We have many choices that we can make every day of our lives, but we should not have the choice of abusing our body just because doing so may give us a good feeling for a short while. We are expected to care for this present from God by keeping ourselves as fit as we possibly can. When we eat the right food and exercise regularly, we are telling God something: we are thankful to Him for His greatest gift to us —the gift of life and health.

Q.   *"Why is there so much talk about drugs today?"*

A.   In recent years we have learned about the many people who have become addicted to drugs and have spent years trying to get rid of their addiction, often without success. The power of drugs over many people of all ages is so strong that they lose control over their lives. Not only do they hurt their own lives, but their parents, brothers, and sisters also suffer. Addicts spend much of the day thinking how they are going to get their next "fix." Sometimes they steal in order to support their habit, and young people from good families may enter a life of crime.

Perhaps you can understand why there are so many television commercials warning us never to start with drugs. For this reason also, most schools require children to learn about the danger of drugs at a very early age.

Q.   *"Isn't cigarette smoking as harmful as taking drugs?"*

A.   Many good people are addicted to both cigarettes and drugs and find it difficult to break the habit. Many people get sick and eventually die from the effects both of cigarette smoking and of taking drugs.

There are differences between cigarettes and drugs, however. For example, few cigarette smokers have to steal in order to support their habit. Unlike the users of certain drugs like crack that change our behavior, the minds of cigarette smokers are not affected.

Q.   *"Does God care if I use drugs or smoke?"*

A.   God can't make us stop hurting our bodies. Only we can make the decision, especially when we become adults. But we can't blame God when we choose to disobey all the warnings.

God is concerned about our making right decisions about our health. He feels saddened when a person of any age refuses His greatest gifts of life and health and answers Him, "No thanks, God, I'll do it my way!"

Q.   *"Is taking drugs something like eating non-*kosher *food?"*

A.   You have hit on an important point. When we talk about *kosher* and non-*kosher*, we usually think of foods that are permitted or prohibited by Jewish Law. However, *kosher* refers also to objects that are fit or unfit for use: A Torah-scroll with letters rubbed out is not *kosher;* the *tefillin* or *mezuzah* that has defective parchment inside it is called non-*kosher* as well and should not be used. In a broader sense, then, *kosher* can mean fit for use and non-*kosher* unfit or off limits.

It would be helpful to expand the term *kosher* to include any food or non-food that improves our health and prolongs our life, and the term non-*kosher* to substances that destroy our health and shorten our life.

❖ *Chapter VI*

JEW AND NON-JEW
"WHY ARE WE DIFFERENT?"

JEW AND NON-JEW

Never before in the history of our people has the Jew in the Diaspora (countries outside of Israel) been so integrated into his or her environment as in America. Despite this fact, however, American Jews are constantly reminded that they are different from their non-Jewish neighbors. These differences are not found to any degree in their appearance, language, or method of living but rather in their religious beliefs and practices, and to some extent in their cultural and social life.

On the Sabbath and holidays many Jews visit their own house of worship; after a day in public school many Jewish children part company with their Christian friends to attend religious school; many Jewish children are absent from class on Jewish holidays.

Judaism has always looked upon the minority status of Jews as an opportunity and a responsibility. Throughout the annals of history, their mere presence as a vibrant minority has given courage and hope to other minorities who have rejected the convenience of conformity for the dignity of freedom—the freedom to think, to worship, and to act independently.

Despite the tragic consequences that have often attended their minority status, Jews have felt that they were prepared to meet the challenges of the enemy, for they were convinced that their forebears had made a convenant with God; they would be loyal to Him and He, in turn, would protect them.

In fact, they felt that oppression would have the effect of ennobling them even more, just as the oil of the olive is produced only after pressing. As long as they were God's instrument for bringing His word to the world, they could accept their role of the "suffering servant."

Because Jews looked upon themselves as members of the "chosen people," they felt a sense of profound humility rather than arrogance. To think that God demanded such a burdensome task of them, to spread His word to the rest of humanity, gave Jews a sense of awesome responsibility and even inadequacy which they almost feared to undertake. As the prophet was to Israel, Israel was in relation to the world—seized by the sense of duty to serve as an instrument of God.

Being chosen did not necessarily imply a feeling of superiority over the other peoples of the world. Jews knew that the Greeks were endowed with a genius for philosophy and science that they did not possess, the Romans were masters of law and administration, the Arabs excelled in poetry and song (areas in which the Jew felt a gnawing sense of inadequacy). But they also knew that they had a special predilection for religion and ethics which could not be disputed. Jews were able to take pagan myths and spiritualize them, and impart great religious concepts to primitive tribal ceremonies. They knew how to live the good life even though many may have strayed far from it.

When the Jews constituted a majority in Biblical Israel, they were enjoined to display more than mere tolerance for the outsider. "One law and one ordinance shall be both for you and for the stranger that sojourns with you." "The stranger that dwells with you shall be unto you as one born among you, and you shalt love him as yourself, for you were strangers in the land of Egypt; I am the Lord your God." These are not to be understood as casual sentiments, since the same thought is repeated no less than thirty-six times in the Pentateuch.

Only a minimum of religious duties were imposed on the non-Jew, such as hearing the Law read once every seven years. This Law did not intend to stimulate conversion but was rather to serve as a reminder to the non-Jew that there were certain laws of the land which every inhabitant was requested to obey. Of course, this feeling of sympathy did not extend to those strangers who were intent upon overthrowing the Israelite government. The Amalekites and Hittites were among those subversive peoples with whom there could be no peaceful coexistence.

Even though our forebears felt that the other religions lacked the spiritual quality of Judaism, it was admitted that they possessed great truths. Righteousness was not the monopoly of religious Jews but could be attained by Gentiles as well. In fact, the righteous of all people were to be granted a portion in the world to come.

It was principally for this reason–the element of goodness common to all religions–that Judaism did not actively seek out converts with the same zeal as did the later Christians and Moslems. They were also apprehensive of non-Jews who sought conversion to Judaism out of some ulterior motive, such as for love of a Jewish woman. Similarly, they feared that the new convert might accept his responsibilities too lightly and might not possess the courage to withstand oppression in times of duress. It should be emphasized that such caution was taken merely to protect and preserve the sanctity of the Jewish religion. Racial exclusiveness was not the intention.

Once the intended convert convinced the rabbi that he wanted to embrace Judaism out of purely idealistic purposes and that he was prepared to cast his lot with his people, no matter what their fate, he was then taught the principles of Judaism leading to his conversion. In fact, God is pictured in the *Aggadah* as expressing even greater love for the *ger* ("convert") who, having chosen Judaism, showed greater qualities than the native Jew, who had not been confronted with such a crucial choice.

Maimonides, the great codifier and philosopher, went as far as to say that the concept of Israel's election was extended to include even the convert. He saw no reason to prevent the convert from including in his daily prayers the invocation "*Our* God and the God of *our* Fathers." He might even thank God for having led *him* out of Egypt.

To be sure, Judaism and Christianity share many similar beliefs:

The Fatherhood of God and the brotherhood of man.

The sanctity of the Hebrew Bible (the *TaNaKH*); to both Christian and Jew its truths are eternal, its insights universal, and its values are indispensable to the good life.

The imperishability of the soul; it is this soul that gives human beings a divine quality, unlike the lower forms of life who were not made in God's image.

Love and understanding of our fellow humans are the supreme goals in life.

However, to minimize the differences between Judaism and Christianity would be to do an injustice to both religions. There are not only ritualistic differences but also a completely different outlook on the nature of God and human beings.

Judaism insists today, as it did before the advent of Christianity, that:

The *Torah* is in itself a fulfillment and does not anticipate a greater fulfillment, a New Testament.

The force for good is more basic to people than the force for evil. We are not burdened at birth with the stigma of Original Sin.

Each person has a direct relationship with God, and there

need be no intermediary man-God to intercede.

Redemption comes through righteous living and the performance of righteous acts (*mitzvot*). People cannot be saved by mere expressions of faith.

Judaism does not, however, repudiate most of the basic teachings of Jesus, the Pharisee. In fact, the master of parable was able to articulate the ethics of Biblical and Talmudic Judaism in a most clear and succinct fashion. Even the religious liberalism of Jesus was not the source of contention. In fact, there were other Jewish teachers who were far more liberal than he in their interpretations of the Law and social doctrine, men who have occupied positions of great esteem in Jewish history.

The real schism came after Jesus' death, when divinity was attributed to him by his followers. It was Paul, a product of the Greco-Roman world, who masterfully breathed into Jesus a new life and new powers that had never been conceived by Jesus the Jew. It was Paul, then, the founder of Christianity, who was responsible for the schism between the two religions, which continued to grow farther apart as Christianity developed.

True, it is possible to find in Jewish writings uncomplimentary remarks and observations about Christianity, most of which, however, are not leveled against Christian doctrine but rather are reactions to accusations leveled against the Jews. Some of the most celebrated Jewish scholars have paid great tribute to Christianity and to its sincere votaries. Judaism has managed to coexist along with other philosophies that were far more inimical to it than Christianity. Jews have merely asked that they be given the opportunity to express and follow their own beliefs and practices without restraint.

"WHY ARE WE DIFFERENT?"

The awareness of being part of a particular religious group comes to the child very early in life, often before school begins. The impact of this awareness of difference from Christian neighbors can affect the Jewish child in many ways. One child will feel unhappy to learn that he is set apart from his neighbors; another will react as if she were superior or exclusive. Or this awareness of difference can resolve itself in a feeling of just pride in being what he is while still respecting his neighbor's convictions. Of course, it is this latter attitude which parents should endeavor to foster among their children. Our children can be taught that to live in two civilizations will bring double enrichment into their lives. There need be no feeling of contradiction between these two cultures, for the American pattern has stressed from its very inception the concept of cultural and religious pluralism, whereby all minorities can remain loyal to their particular traditions without in any way neglecting the national welfare.

Q.   *"What is the origin of the word 'Jew'?"*

A.   The name "Jew" is not found in the *Torah* but appears in the latter books of the Bible. The word comes from Judah or Judaea, the name of the southern kingdom when ancient Palestine was divided after the death of King Solomon. After the destruction of the northern kingdom (Israel), the whole of Palestine was known as Judah and its inhabitants as Jews.

130

Q. "Are the Jews a race?"

A. No. A race is a group of people all of whom can be identified by the same physical characteristics, such as the color of their skin. This is not true of Jews, who belong to every race of mankind.

Q. "Are the Jews called a nation?"

A. No. A nation is a group of people having its own political government. The Jews living in Israel are a nation of Israelis, which includes also the Arabs and Christians who live there. But the Jews who live throughout the world are citizens of the various nations in which they live.

Q. "How then can we refer to the Jewish people?"

A. Jews can best be defined as a people. The members of this people have many things in common of which they are extremely proud—their religion, their culture and history, and their determination to remain a people, or a cultural and religious group.

Q. "Are Jews like one big family?"

A. Yes. We are members of quite a few families. If we were to make a little circle and put a dot somewhere inside, that dot would show us as part of our own immediate family. In a larger circle, that same dot becomes part of a larger family—the Jewish people. And still another larger circle

would show us as part of the American family, while the
largest circle of all shows us as part of the world family,
which includes all human beings.

Q. "How did the Jewish family begin?"

A.   The Jewish family began with the patriarch Abraham. he knew that unless he left his father's country and
started a new people in a new land, he would never be able
to teach his idea of one God to others. So Abraham took his
wife Sarah and a few people whom they influenced, and
went to the land which is now called Israel. This land was
promised to Abraham and to his children by God. To this
very day, Israel has a special meaning to Jews throughout the
world as the cradle of Judaism.

Q. "Why are there many religions?"

A.   Just as most people do not look alike, so do they not
always believe alike. Groups of people–the Christians and
later the Moslems–differed with the religion of the Jews and
started their own groups, though each admitted its great
debt to Judaism.

We in turn respect them for their beliefs; different religions use different roads to reach God.

Q. "What do we mean by religion?"

A.   Religion is a belief in a Being higher than ourselves
who shows us what goals we should strive for in order to be

good. However, religion is not only belief in God and His goals, it is also working toward achieving these goals. It is believing in and doing good that makes one a religious person.

Q. *"Is our religion the best?"*

A. Our religion is the best for us because we know more about it and feel at home with it. We prefer being a member of our family and would not want to be anything different. That does not mean that we are better than our neighbors who have different religious beliefs.

Q. *"Why must Jews do things differently from their neighbors?"*

A. We are different in many ways from our neighbors. One family may sit down to dinner at 6:00 p.m. while a second eats at 7:00. Some children have certain toys that others do not have, and vice versa. Life would be dull if everybody had the same things and did the same thing at one time. This is also true of religious beliefs and customs. It's good to be different, and God is happy if different peoples can still live together and respect one another.

Q. *"What do Jews believe about Jesus?"*

A. The Jews acknowledge that Jesus was born and died a Jew. He studied and taught Judaism as did many other young men of his day. They believe that he was a gifted person who was able to teach the people in such a clear and simple way that everyone understood what he wanted to say.

They do not believe that he alone was the "son of God," who was in any way different from all people who are children of God. Jews do not believe him to be divine (God in human form) or the Messiah destined to save mankind. Many other great Jewish heroes–men like Rabbis Akiba and Hillel–have been greatly revered for their wisdom and their concern for the poor and downtrodden, and yet they were never considered supernatural beings or saviours of mankind.

Q.   *"Is it true that the Jews killed Jesus?"*

A.   No, the Jews did not kill Jesus. His execution was ordered by the Roman Governor, Pontius Pilate, who had many other Jews killed too because they caused trouble to the ruling power and were considered dangerous to the state. Pilate demanded the death of Jesus because he called himself "King of the Jews." To Pilate, this meant one thing–that Jesus was determined to overthrow the power of the Roman king in Judaea and establish himself as the new king.*

---

* Note to Parents: It cannot be emphasized enough that mere factual information will not suffice when a child has been exposed to the accusation that the Jews were responsible for the crucifixion or that they have caused the world's troubles in having rejected the Messiah. The best answer to the troubled child will be found in a sound and wholesome Jewish environment where the child may experience the year-round joy of being a Jew. Kurt Lewin formulated the solution in his penetrating book, *Resolving Conflicts:* "An early build-up of a clear and positive feeling of belongingness to the Jewish group is one of the few effective things that Jewish parents can do for the later happiness of their children. In this way, parents can minimize the ambiguity and the tension inherent in the situation of the Jewish minority group, and thus counteract various forms of maladjustment resulting therefrom."

Q.   *"Why don't Jews celebrate Christmas?"*[†]

A.   Christmas is a Christian celebration commemorating the birth of Jesus. The meaning of the holiday is based on the belief that Jesus was divine, God in human form. Christmas, therefore, has no significance for Jews since one of the basic differences between Judaism and Christianity centers around this question of the divinity of Jesus.

Q.   *"Is it out of place to send a card or gift to a non-Jewish friend at Christmas time?"*

A.   It is certainly appropriate to show a Christian friend that you are thinking of him or her at holiday time. Any way that you can help friends celebrate their own religious holidays should be encouraged. You may volunteer to deliver a friend's newspapers on his religious holiday, a very friendly gesture.

However, it is not appropriate to send Christmas cards or gifts to Jewish friends. When you do, you are encouraging your Jewish friends to accept Christmas or Easter as everyone's holiday, which it is not.

---

† Note to Parents: Both children and parents have often asked about the decoration of the Christmas tree in the Jewish home, an activity that to the uncritical mind has no religious significance. The sensitive Christian is justifiably resentful of the Jew who uses his ceremonial objects for secular purposes. What would be the reaction of most Jews if a Christian took a *Magen David* (for which there is no inherent religious meaning but for which Jews have a great emotional attachment) and used it for amusement purposes? Both the Star of David and the Christmas tree help to create a religious atmosphere and serve to remind Jew and Christian respectively of something more significant than the mere object.

ANTI-SEMITISM
"WHY DO SOME PEOPLE HATE?"

Chapter VII

ANTI-SEMITISM

Leopold Zunz wrote in 1885: "If there are ranks in suffering, Israel takes precedence over all the nations; if the duration of sorrows and the patience with which they are born ennoble, the Jews can challenge the aristocracy of every land; if a literature is called rich in the possession of a few classic tragedies, what shall we say to the National Tragedy lasting for fifteen hundred years, in which the poets and actors were also the heroes?"

Fear and hatred of the Jews can be traced back to their sojourn in Egypt, even before they were welded into a people. The Pharaoh feared them because of their growing numbers; he did not trust them, for he suspected that they would collaborate with the enemy.

The Book of Esther records one of the root causes of anti-Semitism which still obtains today. Haman speaks to King Ahasuerus: "There is a certain people scattered and dispersed among the other peoples in all the provinces of your realm, whose laws are different from those of any other people and who do not obey the king's laws; and it is not in Your Majesty's interest to tolerate them." It is clearly a case of "disliking the unlike" that motivated Haman to seek the annihilation of the Jews. Down the ages people have been anxious to suppress that which they do not understand; and the Jew, who has maintained a unique way of life, has evoked the hostility of the majority.

In the preceding chapter, mention was made of the religious basis for anti-Semitism. In spite of the progress that has been made to create a more positive image of the Jew, the Jew has still not been completely exonerated for his "part" in the crucifixion, which is historically highly questionable. Many Christian and Jewish scholars dealing with the period leading up to the death of Jesus have concluded that the Jews could not possibly be held responsible for his execution.

Another interpretation of the hatred of Jews is the scapegoat mechanism, involving the process of transference. The "escape goat" mentioned in the Bible was sent out annually into the wilderness to carry away the sins of the Israelites. Our forefathers believed that they could transfer the guilt of their sins to the innocent goat. In a similar vein, individuals often seek causes other than themselves for failure or disappointment. From time immemorial the Jews have been convenient "whipping boys" for frustrated individuals and groups who find the source of their difficulties in a defenseless minority. The Jew has been chauvinist, internationalist, communist, capitalist all rolled into one, depending on the particular requirement of the bigot at any given time.

Another psychological cause for anti-Semitism has been cited by Maurice Samuel, noted Jewish author, in *The Great Hatred*. The anti-Semites, he claims, detest the Jews because they gave Jesus to the world, thus imposing a code of morality upon them which they resent. If it were not for the demands of Christianity, for which the Jews are responsible, the Christian would have been able to live a more uninhibited life.

Professor Gordon Allport of Harvard offers a similar explanation for anti-Semitism in his book *The Nature of Prejudice:* "On the one hand people admire and revere these standards, on the other hand they rebel and protest. Anti-Semitism arises because they are irritated by their own conscience. Jews are symbolically their super-ego and no one likes to be ridden so hard by his super-ego. They discredit those people that produced such high ideals."

Ignorance is perhaps the largest contributing factor to anti-Semitism. The untutored person does not hesitate to generalize from one single experience even though facts can disprove the accusation. It is much simpler to claim that *all* Jews are clannish, loud, or mercenary than to abide by the facts. Many years ago the philosopher Spinoza remarked: "If a man has been affected painfully by anyone...the man will feel hatred not only to the individual stranger but also to the whole class or nation to which he belongs."

But the ignorant by no means hold a monopoly on bigotry. Even people trained in scientific method, knowing very well the value of dealing with tangible facts, will sometimes understand best the "facts" that serve their own advantage or document what they already believe. Historians, Bible critics, and poets alike have often joined hands in blaming the Jew for the world's ills. Some have extolled Judaism but denigrated the Jewish people as if they were distinct entities; others have assailed Jewish parochialism in contrast with the "universal spirit of Christianity." The Jewish God has been described by certain scholars as a God of vengeance inspiring fear rather than love in the hearts of people. The Old Testament has been severely criticized for extolling war, encouraging slavery, and advocating irrational punishment for ritual neglect. Unfortunately, such scholars have become emotional when discussing Jews and Judaism. It is interesting to note that some of the most convincing repudiations of this "higher anti-Semitism" have been written by great Christian scholars such as George Moore, Herman Strack, Herbert Danby, and Travers Herford—men who have delved into original Jewish sources in order to find the true spirit of Judaism.

Because of the variety of its causes, it is plain that prejudice cannot be eliminated by any single method. Some experts suggest legislation against anti-Semitism. However, experience has indicated that law cannot change a heart in which prejudice resides; the Soviet Union today has laws against anti-Semitism and so did pre-Hitler Germany. It is fallacious to think that mere facts and figures about Jewish gifts to the world, our indispensability to America, our heroism in the wars can convert the anti-Semite.

It is also certain that if Jews were to withdraw from public life so that they would not be subject to undue criticism, as has been suggested by certain of our own apologists, they would still be vulnerable to attack. The bigot would then be in a position to accuse us for lack of loyalty and indifference to American institutions.

It is primarily a problem of convincing ourselves that Judaism is worthy of survival. Self-acceptance is a prerequisite for acceptance by the outside world. The Jew must be convinced that despite anti-Semitism the intrinsic worth of Judaism demands our survival as a people. Only then can we build up a wall of immunity against the "slings and arrows" of bigotry. The rabbis understood the problem and its solution when they expressed the thought that only when the voice of little children can be heard in the classroom would the "hands of Esau" become impotent. Jewish education then can best fortify the Jew against his enemy, for he not only learns to answer the bigot but, what is more important, how to answer himself.

Status, too, is a powerful antidote to bigotry. It helps not only to engender a sense of genuine pride among the minority, but also to alter the majority opinion. Having no homeland for centuries, the Jews were regarded as parasites; they were one of the few people on earth without a homeland. People who distrusted bi-loyalty accused them of being less patriotic, less honorable in their adopted land than they should be. With the reestablishment of the State of Israel as a spiritual center of world Jewry and with the strengthening of the concept of Jewish peoplehood, the problem of anti-Semitism has been measurably improved. Even where it does exist, it is no longer respectable.

Yet it is still important to fight back against the anti-Semite. Jews should exercise courage and candor in exposing the chronic bigot before all fair-minded people. Moreover, we should expect all freedom-loving people, regardless of their beliefs or affiliations, to help eliminate the corrosive effect of intolerance against the Jew.

"WHY DO SOME PEOPLE HATE?"

How are attitudes toward other people learned? Undoubtedly the home influence has priority as a teacher, and parents can expect children to adopt their own ethnic attitudes ready-made.

At times a child will adopt prejudices from his or her parents, taking on their negative attitudes. Words and gestures as well as superstitions and antagonisms are transferred almost unknowingly to the child. The parents' method of handling the child can develop in the child suspicions, fears, and hatreds that may be directed toward minorities. Studies have shown, for example, that in a home where parents are excessively harsh, suppressive, or critical–where the parents' word is "law"–the soil becomes fertile for group prejudice on the part of the child. Such children are on their guard. They learn that authority dominates human relationships–not trust and tolerance. They learn to mistrust their own impulses, and through the simple act of projection they come to fear evil impulses in others. "They have evil designs and are not to be trusted."

Children who feel secure and loved usually develop basic ideas of equality and trust. Not required to repress their own impulses, they are less likely to transfer them to others and to develop fear and suspicion.

When does prejudice start? Four-year-olds may form in-group feelings excluding other children. A bigoted person may well be in the making by the age of six. At that age racial name-calling is not uncommon; at eight, clubs may be organized excluding certain racial or religious groups. Upon entering school the Jewish child may already be confronted with separation from the majority group.

It is not at all uncommon for a young child to come into the house crying, "Johnny doesn't want to play with me because he says I'm a Jew." Sometimes the child's closest friend will utter insulting words if provoked in an argument. Usually at that age, the "aggressor" is not even aware of what he is saying since the term "Jew" has no meaning to him. He may have heard his parents refer to "the Jewish child" without any malice intended. The child may have intended to distinguish between his friend and himself with whom he was momentarily angry. He could as well say to a little girl playmate, "I don't want to play with you because you are a girl."

There is usually no cause for parental alarm, since the children usually become friends again. It is not wise for the parent of the offended child to get in touch with the other parent unless such taunting persists. If it does, then perhaps a frank discussion with the child's parent might be advisable.

An explanation to one's young child is in order, however, even after the first encounter:

"Johnny, like all of us, sometimes gets angry and he doesn't know what he is saying. Just as you have said things that you really don't mean to your little sister when you get angry, Johnny tries to hurt you for the moment that he was angry. He'll probably be sorry tomorrow."

Older children who have encountered name-calling can be told: "Johnny should really know better. In fact, he is really hurting himself more than you because you will probably forget what he has said in a few days, but he will find himself with fewer and fewer friends if he keeps it up."

It cannot be emphasized enough that the home that helps to prepare the child for Jewish living teaches the child to withstand the taunts of the anti-Semite and to understand his or her own aggressive tendencies toward others. As we have been taught regarding bodily health, an ounce of prevention is worth a pound of cure; similarly, in regard to the child's security, positive Jewish experience in the formative years should be valued more than spending one's adult life combatting anti-Semitism. We must first convince ourselves that Judaism has something to offer us before we can convince our neighbors that Jews have something to offer to them.

Q. "Is the blood of Jews different?"

A.   Hitler felt that Jews had inferior blood but this claim has been disproved by the greatest scientists. There is no difference between the blood of a Christian or Jew, a black or white person. In spite of the fears that still persist, when a healthy black person donates blood to a white person, or a healthy white person donates to a black person, nothing can happen to the patient other than his or her chances for getting well are greatly increased.

Q. "Should a Jew tell his Christian friends that he is Jewish, or should he let them find out for themselves?"

A.   It is advisable to let our non-Jewish friends know from the very outset to which religious group we belong. We should realize that non-Jews will probably respect us more for proudly revealing our Jewishness. If they don't, then they are not worthy of our friendship.

Q. "How should a Jew deal with someone who has attacked him personally?"

A.   It all depends on who the offender is. If he is the type that will not listen to reason, then someone whom he respects or admires—parent, teacher, coach, or minister—should be informed of his constant jibes. If this does not help, then the offender should be exposed before his friends; every attempt should be made to isolate him from other people whom he needs for companionship. Perhaps in this way we may cause him to reconsider his blind prejudice. At any rate we shall have kept our own self-respect in knowing that we have fought back.

If the offender can be reasoned with, then we should take the time to sit down and talk with him about his feelings. Show him how he will suffer more than those whom he talks against by having to live with a troubled conscience. Appeal to his sense of fair play, his desire to be a loyal American.

Q. *"What should a Jew do if the Jewish group is attacked in his presence?"*

A. A Jew may answer in the following way: "Aren't you really unfair to the Jewish people? If you knew more about Jews, you would not be so quick to condemn them. We are human beings who make mistakes like all other humans, no matter to which group they belong. We err not because we are Jews but because we are human beings. You may think I am different. Well, I am different just as you are different from every other person in your group. In fact, no two people in the world are the same nor do they react in the same way to a situation.

Q. *"Why are Jews picked on so much?"*

A. The Jews have been greatly misunderstood. There are people who feel that the Jew is the cause of all their troubles, when usually we are not in the least responsible. When we fall over a chair we may feel like kicking the chair or cursing it even though we should know that the chair was not to blame. So the Jew has been a convenient outlet for criticism, particularly when things are not going well.

Then, too, Jews are disliked and feared by some people merely because they are different. Some people feel the same about Japanese, blacks, or Hispanics because they are unlike the majority of their neighbors. Of course, such people do not understand that it is the right to be different that makes for a living democracy; without that right we would have a dictatorship in this country which would demand that everyone think and act alike.

Q. "Are all non-Jews anti-Semites?"

A.   Few human beings are entirely free from some prejudice, but certainly there are many people who have taken the trouble to find out the truth about Jews and other minorities. They have learned to judge us individually as we should judge them. They do not blame the group for the mistakes of the individuals. Those who have had many contacts with Jews and those who have lived among them will learn to look upon them as naturally as they look upon members of their own group. *

---

* Note to Parents: What has been said about anti-Semitism does not preclude the existence of prejudice among Jewish children. Because of deep-seated feelings of inferiority or outright feelings of exclusiveness, our young people may employ names and tactics that reveal poor attitudes.

"He's just a *goy*" is not an uncommon expression used half innocently by thoughtless people. Parents should constantly examine their attitudes toward other groups; and it goes without saying that they should exercise caution in their use of language either in private or in the presence of their children. If they do hear expressions of this kind, they should explain immediately that if we want others to respect us, we must give them equal respect.

Q. "What does goy *mean?"*

A.   The term *goy* really means "nation" in Hebrew. At one time it was applied to the Jewish people; it carried with it a great deal of dignity. Now it is a slang expression applied to non-Jews.

Q. "How should Jews feel about black people?"

A.   Jews should consider it a moral duty to defend the blacks or any other group when they are attacked, to work toward equality for all people, and to support causes that are dedicated to human equality and civil rights. And Jews should expect the same support from other groups that they are willing to give. We should keep in mind that even though the blacks belong to a different race, their safety and our safety are tied up together. We should never lead ourselves to think that one minority can remain safe as long as another minority is made to suffer from discrimination.

❖ *Chapter VIII*

DEATH
"WHAT HAPPENS WHEN WE DIE?"

Chapter VIII

DEATH

It is only natural that one of the most ancient people on the face of the earth has been vitally concerned with the phenomenon of death. Yet we do not find in the Jewish tradition nearly the same degree of preoccupation with death as existed, for example, among the ancient Egyptians or Persians. Professor George Foote Moore has found a plausible explanation for this difference in emphasis. He explained that among the ancient Jews the prophets were more responsible for the development of Judaism than were the priests. Whereas these prophets were concerned mainly with the affairs of this world and not the future life, among the ancient Egyptians and Persians the priesthood, whose members were most influential in the development of their religious life, developed a highly organized theology centering around death and the afterlife.

Until the Jewish people experienced their first national disaster in 586 B.C.E., there was not even a definite Jewish viewpoint on immortality. In fact, the Books of Job and Ecclesiastes, though denying life beyond the grave, were nevertheless accepted in the Biblical canon. Only later in Jewish history, when the problem of reward and punishment played a more important part in the life of the Jew, did theories about death and the afterlife arise.

Even as late as Talmudic times, Jews were exhorted not to spend too much time on speculation about the future world. The Talmud states explicitly: "Everyone who meddles with the following four things, it were better for him had he not come into this world–what is above, beneath, before, and after."

What then can be said about the basic Jewish attitude toward death? Death is considered to be a natural extension of life when the soul returns to God from whence it originally came.

That is why the traditional Jewish funeral service is noted for its lack of drama; to this day it is simple and unadorned. Music and flowers are omitted. A simple pine box rather than an elaborate coffin is stipulated. The deceased is clothed in plain shrouds. When burial takes place on a holiday or on the New Moon (Rosh Hodesh), eulogies are not delivered over the departed. Death is not to be considered the last stage of existence but a prelude to a new stage of life.

Nevertheless, because life is so precious and so sacred, we seldom find a spirit of resignation among Jews such as is experienced among some other religious groups. It is for that reason, perhaps, that one will occasionally observe emotional outbursts at Jewish funerals. This seemingly paradoxical approach to death was beautifully synthesized by Rabbi Milton Steinberg in one of his sermons, entitled "To Hold with Open Arms." He reminds us that "life is dear; let us then hold it tight while we yet may; but we must hold it loosely also."

It is proper to mourn the loss of a dear one for a year, the most intense period being the first seven day (shivah). For a period of thirty days there is a less intense period of mourning during which one may return to regular chores, though very mindful of the loss one has endured. Then comes the period of ten months marked by adjustment to the new life without the departed, and abstention from certain frivolous pleasures. Joshua Loth Liebman in Peace of Mind calls this period a "hierarchical order in the process of mourning." Judaism wisely provides the mourner with an opportunity to give free expression to his or her emotions at a time when repression could lead to serious psychic disturbances in the years to come.

After the expiration of a year it is considered improper to continue mourning over the loss of one's kin. One must rather learn to readjust oneself to a new life, ever mindful of the loss yet prepared to accept the will of God, who is the true Judge.

In Judaism a variety of opinions have been expressed on the question of life after death. Primarily, immortality has meant that the imperishable soul survives after the flesh, of which it is independent. Just as God gives us the soul at birth, so does He take it back after death. The soul has been described as a "loan" from the great Oversoul, who is God.

Another theory about life and death is that we live on through our children. Just as our children receive our physical characteristics and transmit them to future generations, so do they immortalize us through the heritage that we transmit to them. The rabbis ask: "Why does the Bible state, 'And David slept with his fathers' and not 'David died'? Because David left a son who walked in his ways and continued his noble deeds. Therefore, he is not really dead but has lived on through the good deeds of his successor."

We also live on through the group to which we belong. When Moses protested to God that he did not want to die, God said that His intention was to allow Moses to die so that Israel might live.

When Judaism speaks of immortality, it includes all of these concepts. But primarily immortality means that we are more than flesh and bones; part of the human being, namely the soul, transcends mortality and continues in a different realm of existence.

As to the form of the hereafter, whether there is a Heaven for the righteous or a Hell for the wicked—on this, as on so many other articles of belief, there is no consistent or compelling theology. In fact, tradition has perhaps allowed more latitude on this subject than on any other. Suffice it to say that until the destruction of the First Temple in 586 B.C.E. there was no need for Jews to concern themselves with reward and punishment beyond the grave. Only after the destruction of Jerusalem, when the glory of the Jewish nation seemed doomed, did Jews demand a plausible answer for their suffering. At least in the future world, they reasoned, Jews would be rewarded for their righteousness, and the heathens punished for their wrongdoings.

Out of this concept of group reward developed the doctrine of individual reward and punishment beyond the grave. Rabbi Israel Levinthal, writing on the subject in *Judaism, An Analysis and Interpretation,* indicates that "the Jew did not even have a conception of Heaven and Hell as concrete places for reward and punishment, that he had to borrow even his vocabulary for such designations from places on earth." The Hebrew term by which Paradise is designated is *Gan Eden,* "the garden which God planted on earth." Later, *Gan Eden* came to mean otherworldly bliss. *Gehenna,* too, which came to mean Hell, was originally a place on earth where the wicked sacrificed their children to Moloch.

We find the basic Jewish viewpoint toward life and death most eloquently expressed in the *Kaddish.* The *Kaddish,* which is recited by the mourner, is not at all a prayer for the dead. In fact, neither the deceased nor his or her passing is mentioned. It is rather an expression of faith in God even when we must suffer by His judgment. It is, in a sense, an affirmation by the living to take up the burden of life from those who bear the burden no longer. Its theme is not the world beyond, but "May He establish His kingdom during your life and during your days, and during the life of all the house of Israel."

"WHAT HAPPENS WHEN WE DIE?"

It is impossible to shield the child from the reality of death once the child has reached age three or four. The realization of it may come with the death of a pet dog or the sight of a dead insect. Even casual use of the word "death" in the child's presence arouses curiosity as to what the parents mean.

It is difficult to explain the concept of death to the very young child. We may, however, be able to spare our children a great deal of anxiety in later life by preparing them to confront this inevitable stage in human development. Furthermore, children can be taught that while accepting the inevitability of death, they should consider life so much dearer because it does not last forever.

Parents are often reluctant to have their children attend a funeral or visit a house of mourning. It is true that these experiences may create indelible impressions, but why shouldn't they? We should not expect our young ones to live in a world of fantasy when their happiness requires their ability to accept reality. If our explanation is satisfying to them, they will learn to benefit by their experience. Surprisingly, children can be of great comfort to us when we have lost our dear ones just as we can help them immeasurably in their understanding of death. They want to share in our experience as they want us to share in theirs.

When death occurs within a family, some of us may think that we are doing the child a favor by helping to distract the child. We may feel that we should provide exciting entertainment or surround the child with friends who will help him or her forget this harrowing experience, but these palliatives are as ineffective for children as they are for adults. When we look for escape and try "to get away from it all" we can rest assured that sooner or later our grief will catch up with us. The child needs an older person who will listen patiently and help the child through this turbulent period. The sorrow will not necessarily be forgotten, but at least the child will be spared the feelings of loneliness and helplessness that often attend experiences of death.

Let us guard if possible against using platitudes to discuss the deceased; these are not only empty of meaning but can create a harmful effect on the child's thinking. Someone might carelessly say, "It would be selfish of us to wish him back when God needs him more." Such remarks may create bitterness toward God in later life, for the child will feel repressed feelings of guilt for being selfish. It is impossible to measure the extent of antagonism that has developed toward religion because of well-meaning yet careless remarks by parents.

The child's courage in the presence of death is determined largely by the extent of the parents' faith in God—a faith that can help the child muster stamina and strength to meet the trials of life.

Q.   *"When grandpa died, where did he go?"* *

A.   Grandpa is not with us any longer, but he has gone to live in a wonderful place where no one is sick or feels pain. To live is wonderful, but none of us can live forever, just as spring and summer cannot last forever.

*   Note to Parents: The picture of death calling to man is beautifully allegorized by Joshua Loth Liebman in *Peace of Mind*. This can be effectively related to the young child: "You know that after you have played a full day in the park on a summer day I call you in to be with me; so does God call His children after a full life to be in His presence once again. Now you wouldn't want grandfather to suffer or to be in pain! He doesn't suffer any longer." We can indicate what a wonderful life he had, that he built a fine home and brought up children who married and had families of their own.

To delude the child into thinking that his grandfather took a long trip to Hawaii, hoping that this will satisfy the child, solves practically nothing. The child is not learning how to accept the phenomenon of death and, furthermore, is being told something that eventually he will have to reject.

Q. *"Will he ever come back?"*

A. No, a person who dies never comes back, but that does not mean that we cannot love him and think of him.

Q. *"When are you going to die?"* †

A. I will die some day, of course, but we do not know when. Nobody knows. However, I will probably be here for a good long time, and by then you will be grown up with a family of your own.

Q. *"If I speak to grandpa, will he hear me?"*

A. Probably not, but God with whom grandpa now rests hears you, and He is always ready to hear what you say about grandpa. God wants to know that you love him and that you miss him greatly.

† Note to Parents: The child is not necessarily expressing a conscious or unconscious wish in posing this question but is endeavoring to understand more fully the meaning of death.

Q. *"Why do some children die?"* *

A.   We have read short stories and long stories, we have sung songs of few words and songs of many stanzas. We do not measure the greatness of any story or song by its length; sometimes one word spoken at the right time can mean more than a book of words. So life cannot always be measured only by how long we live. Some people live until they are eighty, and they do little good for themselves or for others, and at times a boy or girl can do wonderful things in the seven or eight years of life that God has given to him or her.

Note to Parents: The following story taken from the Talmud may be told effectively to children who inquire about the passing of young people:

While Rabbi Meir was holding his weekly lesson in the House of Study one Sabbath afternoon, his two beloved sons died suddenly at home. The grief-stricken mother carried them to her room and covered them with a sheet. When Rabbi Meir returned after the evening services, he asked his wife Beruriah about the boys, whom he had missed in the synagogue. Instead of replying, she asked him to recite the *Havdalah* service marking the departure of the Sabbath, and gave him his evening meal. When it was over, Beruriah turned to her husband and said: "I have a question to ask you. Not long ago, some precious jewels were entrusted to my care. Now the owner has come to reclaim them. Shall I return them?

"But of course," said the rabbi. "You know the Law." Beruriah then took him by the hand, led him to the bed, and drew back the sheet. Rabbi Meir burst into bitter weeping. "My sons, my sons!" he lamented. Then Beruriah reminded him tearfully: "Did you not say that we must restore to the Owner what He entrusted to our care? Our sons were the jewels which God left with us and now their Master has taken back His very own."

Q. *"Why must people die at all?"*

A. Death really makes new life possible. If there were no such thing as death, eventually there would be no room for birth on this earth. The world would be so crowded that everyone would be scrambling for space and food to keep alive. Someone has figured out that if only one kind of insect, the locust, were to live forever and continue to breed, they would soon crowd every plant off the face of the earth. As a result the locusts themselves would eventually die because they would have no food. The same would happen if people lived forever.

Besides, think of the time we would waste if we knew we were going to live forever. We would not think about making the most out of each day. The thought that our life must eventually come to an end makes us appreciate every day that much more.

Q. *"Does any part of us still exist after death?"*

A. We choose to think that part of us remains alive; we believe that the soul lives on, the soul that God lends to us when we are born. This part of us does not die with the body because it belongs to God, and it eventually returns to Him.

The following story may help you understand what we mean. A little boy found a bird nest which contained speckled eggs. He looked at it continually. Then one day he had to take a trip to the city. Upon his return, he rushed to the nest to see the eggs. He was shocked to find that the beautiful eggs were broken. All he saw were empty shells. He wept before his father, "These beautiful eggs are spoiled and broken." "No, my son," answered his father, "they're not spoiled. The best part of them has taken wings and flown away."

Q.   *"How do you know that the soul lives on forever?"*

A.   We don't know for sure that this is true, but many people have faith that it does. They believe that since the soul is part of God in us, it lives on forever, since no part of God can be destroyed. They do not believe that the soul depends on the body for its existence. It is amazing how many persons who are totally disabled because of disease or sickness still have such wonderful minds and high spirits. For instance, there was a great man by the name of Franz Rosenzwieg, whose entire body was paralyzed; he could move only one finger and nothing else. Yet, his mind was so great and his will so strong that he was able to dictate some of his greatest thoughts to his wife by the mere tapping of his finger through a code system. One cannot help but believe that there was a great spirit in him distinct from his disabled body.

Q.   *"What do we mean by faith in a future life?"*

A.   When we believe in something very much without being able to prove it, that is faith. When Columbus set out on his first voyage from the shores of Spain, he was not sure what was beyond the vision of his eye, but he had faith that the great sea had another shore. Similarly, we cannot see beyond this life, but we do believe that another life does exist.

Index